# GUILT
# AND
# FREEDOM

Bruce Narramore
and
Bill Counts

VISION HOUSE PUBLISHERS
Santa Ana, California 92705

ACKNOWLEDGEMENTS

*The authors express their appreciation to Mrs. Joyce Sinclair, diligent secretary and gracious typist of this manuscript.*

Scriptures from the following translations are used by permission of the copyright owners:

*Amplified Bible,* © 1964 Zondervan Publishers, © 1958 the Lockman Foundation.
*The New Testament in Modern English, by J. B. Phillips,* © 1958 J. B. Phillips, Macmillan Publishing Company, N.Y., N.Y.
*New American Standard Bible, and New Testament,* © 1960, 1962, 1963, 1968, 1971 the Lockman Foundation.
*Revised Standard Version,* © 1946, 1952 the Division of Christian Education of the National Council of Churches.
*The Living Bible,* © 1971 Tyndale House Publishers.

Quotations from the following copyrighted books are printed by the kind permission of the owners:

*Born Crucified,* by L. E. Maxwell, © 1945 Moody Press, Moody Bible Institute of Chicago.
*The Calvary Road,* by Roy Hession, © 1950 Christian Literature Crusade, London, England, and Fort Washington, Pa.
*Commentary on the Epistle to the Galatians,* by Martin Luther, abridged and translated by Theodore Graebner, © 1949 Zondervan Publishing House, Grand Rapids, Mich.
*Handbook of Happiness,* by Charles Solomon, © 1971, Grace Fellowship Press, Denver, Colo.
*A History of the Modern World,* by Robert R. Palmer and Joel Colton, © 1953 Alfred A. Knopf, Inc., N.Y., N.Y.
*Jonathan Livingston Seagull,* by Richard Bach, © 1970 Richard D. Bach, Macmillan Publishing Company, N.Y., N.Y.
*Toward a Psychology of Being,* by Abraham Maslow, © 1968 D. Van Nostrand Company, N.Y., N.Y.
*Why I Am Not A Christian* and other essays on religion and related subjects, by Bertrand Russell and others, © 1956 Simon and Schuster, N.Y., N.Y.

GUILT AND FREEDOM

# Contents

1 GUILTY—WHO, ME?      7
*Thousands "End It All" ... We Can't Escape ...
Guilt, the Couch, and the Pulpit ... "I Blew It!"*

2 THE GREAT MASQUERADE      11
*"I Work Best Under Pressure" ... "I'm Just Shy"
... "I Can't Say No" ... The Constant Critic ...
Sex Hang-Ups ... Money Gets You Either Way ...
Freedom Now*

3 THE BIRTH AND GROWTH OF GUILT      19
*Your Ideal-Self ... Your Punitive-Self*

4 THE GREAT GUILT FAILURE      27
*Guilt Games ... Guilt's Total Failure ... Does the
Bible Promote Guilt?*

5 WHO AM I, REALLY?      38
*The Roots of Self-Esteem ... "I'm a Perfect,
Unlimited Seagull" ... "I'm a Lowly, Wretched
Worm" ... "Who Am I, Really?"*

6   THE LIBERATED SELF                                52
*The Identity Crisis . . . Your Personal Civil War . . .*
*Self-Denial That Isn't . . . Self-Denial That Is . . .*
*How Inferiority Masquerades as Pride . . . How*
*Inferiority Masquerades as Humility . . . True*
*Humility . . . Self-Liberation . . . Practical Hints*
*Toward Self-Liberation . . . "Doing What Comes*
*Naturally"*

7   THE I O U COMPLEX                                 66
*Does God Punish Wrongdoing? . . . Was This the*
*Final Payment? . . . Discipline or Punishment? . . .*
*Respect and Fearful Anxiety . . . Rewards*

8   THE SILENT TREATMENT                             76
*The Ninety Percent Hero and Five Percent Flop . . .*
*One Way of Acceptance*

9   "IF I BELIEVED ALL THAT . . . "                  86
*Those Wild Oats . . . No Man Is an Island . . . Why*
*Be Good?*

10   GOOD OLD GRACE                                  94
*Two Ways . . . The Two Will Never Mix . . . Lapsing*
*Back Under Law . . . Why Do We Do All This?*

11   LEGALISM LIES ON THE COUCH                     107
*That Hidden Childish Fear . . . The law Isn't Useless*
*. . . Legalism Is Opposed to Law!*

12   WHAT DO YOU DO WHEN YOU BLOW IT?               118
*Who Says You Blew It? . . . What's the Real Prob-*
*lem? . . . Who Is Your Accuser? . . . God's Alter-*
*native to Psychological Guilt . . . The Continuing*
*Guilt Battle*

13   TRUE CONFESSIONS                               128
*Confession and Catharsis . . . Abuses of Confession*
*. . . Avoid It Like the Plague*

14   DECISIONS, DECISIONS!                     **138**
     *Three Ways To Go . . . Doubtful Things in Corinth
     . . . First Century Group Therapy . . . What Makes
     Grace Work*

15   "BUT THAT'S NOT WHERE MY HEAD IS!"        **150**
     *What's Your Route? . . . Toward Freedom and
     Stability*

# 1

# Guilty--Who, Me?

In the spring of 1959 an Air Force major entered a Texas mental institution for the second time. He had tried to commit suicide twice and he had been arrested for forgery and robbery. For years he had been drinking heavily and his marriage had disintegrated. Yet only fifteen years before, he had been a model officer headed for a promising career.

One momentous event precipitated the major's plunge. He flew the lead plane over Hiroshima when the first atom bomb was dropped. Shortly afterward he began seeing throngs of Japanese men, women, and children chasing him in his dreams, and his own life began to collapse. The psychiatrist who treated him said the major was subconciously trying to provoke punishment from society to atone for the guilt he felt over Hiroshima and other acts. Unresolved guilt was destroying his life.

Few of us suffer such grievous guilt, but all of us are troubled occasionally by recurring pangs of hidden guilt. Guilt, self-acceptance, and inner freedom are problems for all of us.

## Thousands "End It All"

Some people, torn by a sense of failure and despair, turn to self-destruction. In a year's time 21,000 people in the

United States "end it all." Their guilt, coupled with feelings of isolation and anger turned inward on themselves, propels them to destruction.

For most of us, the conflict is less severe. We aren't battered by wave after wave of depression. We aren't considering suicide. And we do see life as worth living. But even then we aren't entirely free. In moments of quiet reflection, we know we fall short of our hopes and expectations. In spite of our sincere intentions, we rarely measure up to our ideals. We sense an inner, creative potential but are continually falling short of its fulfillment. These shortcomings lead to feelings of guilt that occasionally haunt us all.

Along with guilt, we have another problem—self-acceptance. All of us want to feel good about ourselves. We want to feel important, worthy, and acceptable to others. Most of all, we want to be at harmony with ourselves. We want to believe we are likeable and living up to our potential. But since we fall short at times, we are prone to feelings of failure, worthlessness, and self-rejection. This blocks us from real freedom.

### We Can't Escape

Some people think guilt is no problem for them—they have things well in hand. But frequently this isn't true. Since guilt is a painful feeling, we unknowingly disguise it and hide it from our conscious minds. By pushing it into the unconscious, we think we're free. But our restless emotional lives betray us. We continue to be troubled by inner conflicts and frustrations as the repressed guilt sneaks out under other names.

In spite of our "enlightened society," our "new morality," and our "psychological maturity," our era continues to be plagued by guilt. We have disguised and distorted our experience of guilt so we no longer recognize its presence. But we have only substituted a new vocabulary and a new code for what was previously known as guilt. Parents and teachers who used to say a child was "good" or "bad" now say he is "mature" or "immature" and "adjusted" or "maladjusted." But now these words have taken on the same meaning as the previous "good" or "bad." We feel the old sense of guilt if we aren't "mature" or "well-adjusted."

Thus, in a world plagued by personal frustrations and attended by an army of mental health professionals, many people look for relief from a nameless anxiety without realizing their basic problem is really guilt.

## Guilt, the Couch, and the Pulpit

Coming from different backgrounds and professions, the authors of this book have encountered the problems of guilt and self-acceptance in many settings. One of us is a professional psychologist who has worked extensively to help depressed and guilt-ridden people throw off the oppressive forces of their condemning consciences. The other is a theological seminary graduate who has counseled hundreds of college students whose lives were torn by feelings of guilt and worthlessness.

Personally speaking, both of us at times have been bothered by guilt and a lack of self-acceptance. But it wasn't until a few years ago that we began to study these problems in depth. Team teaching graduate courses in psychology, we discovered how much certain insights of psychology complement the timeless truths of the Bible. We began to gain a new understanding into personality wholeness and found these truths sinking into our own lives to produce a new sense of spontaneity and release.

In putting these thoughts in book form, we hope to take the reader with us through the problems of guilt and self-acceptance to a more relaxed and productive existence. While all growth is a process, we believe the ideas set forth here are key ingredients of a growing, liberated self.

## "I Blew It!"

The most obvious experience of guilt comes when we violate a specific prohibition—either in thought or action. Suddenly we have an inner sense of self-reproach or condemnation. We think, "I blew it; how stupid of me!" Or, "I should have known better!" Sometimes we gain immediate relief by admitting our wrongs or making restitution. Other times it doesn't come so easily. In extreme cases we may be repeatedly haunted by an inner voice reminding us of failure.

This type of guilt feeling is common and generally understood. But it's only one of many forms of guilt. Other forms are far more subtle, so subtle, in fact, that we may not recognize their presence. Let's unmask some of these disguises.

# 2

# The Great Masquerade

When Ann, a minister's wife, came to me for counseling, she was suffering deep feelings of depression. Her self-image was poor and she thought she didn't deserve any of life's pleasures. As often happens, her husband's church responsibilities left him little time for her and the children. Instead of sharing quiet evenings at home or family outings, he was preoccupied with board meetings, visitation, sermon preparation, and church socials. This life-style reinforced Ann's feelings of rejection. Her own needs seemed less important than the needs of the church. Her depression had become so bad that she was considering suicide. She made no attempt on her life but was strongly tempted.

Through counseling, her husband became more aware of her needs and altered his schedule to spend more time with his family. One weekend they planned a trip to Disneyland and Ann thought, "For once we'll be alone."

They arranged for a babysitter and were on their way. But as they approached Disneyland, Ann suddenly felt like jumping from the car and destroying herself. She didn't understand the impulse and became emotionally distraught. They continued on the outing, but their pleasure was ruined.

Later, as we discussed the incident, Ann said sadly, "I guess I feel so worthless that I don't deserve a day at Disneyland." Her feelings were becoming clear; she was

trying to punish herself. Her role as a busy minister's wife
supported this self-punishment. Though she resented the
church's heavy demands, she thought it was her lot in life.
When her husband's attitude changed and her situation im-
proved, she couldn't stand it. She felt she had to pay for
anticipated pleasure with the punishment of suicide. Ann
was experiencing guilt as deep depression, self-punishment,
and feelings of personal worthlessness.

The Bible gives an example of this process. When the chief
priests sought a quiet way to capture Jesus, Judas Iscariot
made a bargain to betray him. For thirty pieces of silver
(about $17), he agreed to single Jesus out by kissing him.
After this extreme deceit, Judas experienced unbearable
guilt. He threw the silver on the temple floor and cried out,
"I have sinned by betraying innocent blood" (Matthew 27:4,
*NASB*). Then he went out and hanged himself.

Few of us have such extreme reactions, but we all have
similar emotions. Some of us find it difficult to experience
pleasure. On weekends and vacations we think we're wasting
time. We find it difficult to relax. Others unconsciously
arrange their lives—even to the point of choosing poor marriage partners or unworthy occupations—so they can punish
themselves. If happiness comes their way, they quickly con-
vert it into misery—often for others as well as for themselves.

Other people are filled with self-blame. When conflicts
arise or mistakes are made, this person takes the blame. Even
when others are clearly in the wrong, they find some way of
turning things around and piling blame on themselves. They
are also unable to accept an honest compliment or expression of affection. They think they "don't deserve it." At the
root of their problems are deep feelings of unresolved guilt.

Some parents teach children that all of life is a duty and
responsibility. Children are told to be self-sacrificing, always
putting others first. When this is overdone, pleasure becomes
an unnecessary luxury. This instills a subtle sense of guilt
with each enjoyable experience. Should they allow some
pleasure, a payment must be made. This payment comes in
the form of guilt.

### "I Work Best Under Pressure"

Some people are unable to operate without pressure. So housework piles up. Studies are put off. Work at the office is deferred. Yardwork is neglected. And personal correspondence sits unanswered.

Take letter writing, for example. We may receive a letter from a friend and appreciate his interest. We *want* to write back soon, but we're busy with something else. In a few days we remember the letter and remind ourselves that we *should* answer, but we put it off again. Still later the letter comes to mind again and we think, "That's me. I'm just irresponsible and ungrateful. If I were a good friend I would have found time to reply before now." Each time the letter comes to mind we condemn ourselves. Soon others join the stack. With each one our sense of guilt and condemnation grows.

Finally the pressure of guilt becomes so great we *must* write to relieve it and we spend hours catching up on correspondence. In this way guilt motivates some of us to action. When little guilt exists, we do nothing. When condemnation builds, it produces pressure like steam in a boiler. We finally get to work, but with much discomfort.

For others, the result of guilt pressure is more devastating. As guilt builds, they are paralyzed. Each task seems so big and the guilt so great they sink in despair. The guilt becomes an insurmountable barrier that continues to grow daily.

### "I'm Just Shy"

At one time or another, most of us have felt tense and ill at ease in a social setting. Perhaps we were the only "outsider" or we didn't know others well enough to be comfortable. When a few people joined in conversation, we felt left out and wished we could be in their group. But we didn't have quite the confidence to walk over, introduce ourselves, and join right in.

Some people experience this isolation acutely. When others look their way, they think, "Maybe they're talking about me." This sensitivity may reflect a hidden guilt. They think (sometimes unconsciously), "If they knew what I'm really like, they wouldn't want me. But perhaps they do know!" This fear stirs up discomforting anxiety. It isn't experienced directly as guilt, but is camouflaged as social insecurity.

The first people on earth experienced this problem. After eating the fruit God specifically forbade, Adam and Eve felt guilt. When God came walking in the garden, they hid. God said, "Where are you?" and Adam replied, "I heard the sound of Thee in the garden, and I was afraid because I was naked; so I hid myself" (Genesis 3:8-10, *NASB*).

### "I Can't Say No"

Some of us have trouble saying "No." Fearing disapproval, we answer every call to help. When a club or church needs a volunteer, we offer to assist. When a charity seeks donations, we always give a little. And when other people expect conformity, we can be counted on to follow.

This unvarying concession reflects a hidden guilt. Although we may say, "There's no one else," or "Someone's got to do it," we're kidding ourselves. Under a cloak of altruism we are forcing ourselves to deny our individual freedom and relaxation times. We can't take time for ourselves for fear of being considered selfish or unkind.

Some people use gifts and social niceties to cover hidden guilt. What husband hasn't brought his wife a special gift after being especially unkind? Or what father hasn't given children presents or money when he knew they really wanted his time? And how often do we give presents to people we hardly know or invite others to dinner even though we'd rather not? In each instance we are motivated partly out of guilt emotions.

The Old Testament gives a clear example of this process. After Jacob cheated his older brother, Esau, out of his father's blessing, he fled the country. Years later, when about to encounter his brother again, Jacob sent lavish gifts to appease his brother's wrath (Genesis 27:1-29; 32:1-5). Guilt was mingled with his instinct for self-preservation.

## The Constant Critic

All of us occasionally turn to judging others. Sometimes we do it to hide our own guilt. Although we try to disguise our judgments as "constructive criticisms" or "Christian concern," our hidden attitude may be very different. By focusing on the faults of others, we can manage to avoid looking at ourselves. Sometimes we're even guilty of the very acts we criticize in others.

The Bible clearly warns us to remove the "beam" from our own eye before searching for the "speck" in our brother's (Matthew 7:3-4) and to avoid criticizing others lest we bring judgment on ourselves (Matthew 7:1-2). Genesis records an example of this condemning attitude (Genesis 38:1-30). Judah, one of Joseph's brothers, unwittingly committed adultery with his own daughter-in-law, a woman named Tamar. This came about when Tamar, whose husband had died, veiled herself and sat by the road like a prostitute to lure Judah into sexual relations. Judah casually complied and promised a goat from his flock in payment, then he left his ring and staff with her as a deposit. Some months later Tamar was found to be pregnant. When this was discovered, she was accused of being a harlot and brought to Judah, the family leader. He immediately said, "Bring her forth and let her be burned." When Tamar appeared, she held up the ring and staff and said, "By the man whose these are, am I with child."

No culprit has ever looked more foolish. Judah had self-righteously condemned his daughter-in-law's immorality when he was fully as guilty. This type of judging and criticism is often present in much less serious situations. It is based on the unconscious projection of our own faults on to others.

## Sex Hang-Ups

In our "enlightened," sexually-sophisticated society, masses of people continue to be plagued with emotional guilt and constrictions over sex. We think our new morality and situational ethics have freed us from our inhibitions, but it isn't true. Many people who have premarital or extra-marital sexual experience claim to be free of guilt and anxiety, but their lives reflect the hidden guilt. Even though they have rationalized their guilt feelings into the unconscious, they fail to experience a sense of personal fulfillment and self-acceptance. In fact, they may suffer from an increased feeling of "split allegiance" from trying to give themselves intimately to too many people.

For many, premarital relationships turn out to be ego-building trips or frantic attempts to fill an inner craving for acceptance. Unexpectedly, these trips have crash landings. The temporary feeling of acceptance and elation gradually crumbles amidst the dying coals of a temporary love relationship.

Many women become sexually frigid after apparently enjoyable premarital relations. Others go from one temporary love affair to another, never able to establish a fulfilling life relationship because of their inner conflict.

Phyllis, a married woman in her thirties, came to me for counseling. She felt no enjoyment in her sexual life. She came from a strongly religious home where sex was a taboo subject. Her parents often commented on the "loose morals," "indecent dress," and "ungodly influence of the world." Occasionally they said that "sex is beautiful in marriage." But the general impression was that sex is dirty. This caused a gap between her intellectual knowledge and her feelings. Her mind said, "Sex is good," but her feelings said, "No, it's dirty."

When she entered marriage as a virgin, Phyllis had some anxiety over sexual intercourse, but assumed she would "get over it." Unfortunately, her feelings hadn't changed after several years of marriage. She instinctively felt sex was wrong and dirty. The only way she could reach a climax was to imagine herself as another woman during intercourse. This pretense temporarily freed her of her inhibitions, but it brought other problems. Her sense of guilt produced a vicious circle.

She thought, "It's my wifely duty to please my husband, but I don't enjoy it." She gave in to his sexual advances but experienced no pleasure. She felt dirty and cheapened, or she accused him of using her as an object or "only having sex on his mind." Her husband also developed a sense of guilt. He knew he had lusted and at times he was more concerned with achieving sexual release than tenderly caring for his wife. Feeling this was selfish, he too suffered pangs of guilt. For both married and single, guilt plays a crucial role in our sexual adjustment.

## Money Gets You Either Way

America is at a pinnacle of world prosperity. No other large nation has such living standards, as much leisure time, and so many luxuries. Yet we haven't found contentment in prosperity. As little children, most of us were told of the starving children in Africa or China. When we failed to clean up our plates, we experienced a twinge of guilt. Why should we be able to waste our food while millions starve?

As adults, we see advertisements for an orphan-relief organization showing a pathetically sick child with her hand outstretched. The ad tells us a few pennies a day will feed her. Again we feel a sense of guilt. Why should we buy a four-hundred dollar television set while millions starve, live in rat-infested ghettoes, or eke out their existence on a few acres of worn-out farmland? We have difficulty enjoying prosperity because of guilt.

At other times we feel guilty over a lack of financial progress. Our culture still judges us partly by financial status. A "successful" man is usually a wealthy man. Husbands under financial pressure often begin to feel guilty for "not providing for their families." When a wife asks for nicer things, she is subtly (or sometimes not so subtly!) saying,

"You're not a good provider." Her husband may react with irritation, or he may keep his cool and give a rational reply. But inwardly he fears she is right—he should be doing better.

### Freedom Now!

So in almost every area of our lives we confront the damage done by guilt. Guilt has a way of binding us down, of pressuring us, and of robbing us of freedom and spontaneity. And none of us is entirely free of guilt's influence. The perfectionist housewife; the worrier; the aggressive, driven businessman; the insomniac; the straight-"A" student; and the searching religious person are all partially motivated by hidden guilt. Each is trying something to develop a sense of self-acceptance or inner harmony. Must we live as slaves to guilt and its various disguises?

The confident message of this book is that we can be free from the inhibiting effects of guilt. While each of us must struggle with our own humanity, we don't have to be tied by the restraints and condemnations of a guilty conscience. Both the Bible and psychology have much to say about guilt and self-acceptance. Freedom from guilt is at the heart of God's plan for the human race, and psychologists have done much to clarify the nature and origin of the guilt problem.

By combining biblical principles with the insights of psychology, we can learn to recognize the subtle influences of hidden guilt when they make their first appearance. Then, through God's principles and the power of new life, we can break guilt's clutch. We can throw off the subtle yet crippling influences of guilt in our everyday lives. We *can* be free!

# 3

# The Birth And Growth Of Guilt

Once I asked five-hundred people to answer the question: "What do you experience when you are feeling guilty?" Their answers reflected a wide range of inner emotions. Here are a few of their responses.

"I'm scared of what's ahead."

"My mind has a tendency to kick itself."

"I have a feeling of impending punishment."

"I feel like a raunchy person—a complete failure."

"I feel unworthy, unvaluable and somewhat inferior."

"Dirty or stained."

"Bitter, like an awful person—sad and sorry."

"I feel terrible—like nobody loves me—especially God."

"I feel dislike for myself, not accepted."

"Separated, like I don't want to show my face to people."

If you look at these statements carefully you see they fall into three categories. The first three statements reflect a *fear of punishment*. The next four reflect a feeling of *depression, worthlessness, and lowered self-esteem*. And the last three reflect a feeling of *isolation and rejection*. These three attitudes form the core of guilt-emotions. Whenever we feel guilty we're actually experiencing an internal fear of punishment, a sense of unworthiness, or a fear of alienation and rejection.

How do these feelings develop? How does the conscienceless infant develop standards and learn to feel guilt? And why do some adults experience guilt so much more strongly than their neighbors? To answer these and other questions, we need to look at how our personalities develop. By looking at the influences that shape our emotional lives, we can begin to unravel the cords of binding guilt.

## Your Ideal-Self

To put it briefly, guilt feelings come when our thoughts or behavior fall short of our ideals. Shortly after birth we begin to develop a set of goals, ideals, and aspirations. We learn that certain behavior is desired and encouraged by our parents. We are instructed to "do this" and "do that." We are taught to obey, say "please," and clean our rooms, and to refrain from fighting, interrupting, and being rude.

Each family has its own set of goals and aspirations. Some families place a high value on musical ability. Others pride themselves on social skills, political beliefs, academic achievement, or financial prosperity.

Personality traits such as introversion and extroversion also have different values in different homes. Ghetto children are often taught to fight to earn their rights. In other families, aggression is discouraged and children are taught to be quiet and conforming. Certain families cherish moral and spiritual values built on Bible study, prayer, church attendance, and "good behavior."

As we grow, we learn other values from our environment. Our American "television culture" values things like physical beauty and athletic stardom. Talk shows and TV specials prize quick wit as an American ideal. More recently, we are placing great importance on social causes. Playmates and teachers hold up other goals and aspirations. Gradually, out of these many possibilities, we evolve our personal ideals. The influence of parents, teachers, schoolmates, and other important people combines to shape these unique standards.

This set of goals is called our ideal-self. By adolescence it has become firmly entrenched within our personalities. Although our values may gradually change with new experience, their basic pattern is well established by our teen-age years. Just as right- or left-handedness, habits of speech, and physical mannerisms are deeply ingrained, our political, social, spiritual, and moral values are also firmly embedded in our personalities. Try as we may, this "ideal-self" is not readily altered.

But there is another inescapable force shaping our deepest selves. The Bible says there is a universal awareness of basic moral standards. In writing of people who don't have God's written laws, the apostle Paul says: "He will punish the heathen when they sin, even though they never had God's written laws, for down in their hearts they know right from wrong. God's laws are written within them; their conscience accuses them, or sometimes excuses them" (Romans 2:14, 15, *TLB*).

No matter what race or culture anthropologists visit, they find this type of law. Every person who has ever lived and every society that has ever existed has had some innate sense of right and wrong. Even in subcultures with low morals and homes where parents fail to give needed moral instruction, children grow up with a general sense of right and wrong. This inner standard silently judges our deeds as a part of our ideal-self.

### Your Punitive-Self

There is also a negative catalyst of the guilt-emotion. While we are adopting some of our parents' ideals, we are also absorbing their disciplinary methods and attitudes toward our misbehavior. In later life—even in the absence of our parents—we automatically tend to repeat their methods of correction on ourselves. Don't we sometimes scold ourselves with the exact words and tones of voice our parents used? This is the voice of our inner parent—our "corrective self."

To the degree our parents used loving, sensitive, constructive discipline, we develop a healthy corrective attitude.

Then when we fall short of our ideals, we acknowledge our failures, empathize with those we've hurt, and plan remedial actions. But to the degree we take in hostile and degrading corrective attitudes, we develop feelings of neurotic guilt.

To understand how guilt feelings are generated, consider what happens when a child misbehaves. Recall what our parents did when we failed to live up to their ideals. Among the possible parental reactions are: (1) punishment in anger or frustration, (2) shaming for misbehavior, (3) subtle rejection for failure.

At one time or another, most of us have frustrated our parents, angered them, or exposed their feelings of inadequacy. When this happened, they may have responded with anger, unnecessary punishment, verbal lashings, or various forms of personal rejection. These parental responses are the seedbeds for emotional guilt. In fact, they correspond exactly to the three elements of the guilt emotion, namely (1) the fear of punishment, (2) feelings of worthlessness or lowered self-esteem, (3) a feeling of alienation or rejection. Let's see how these feelings grow to prominent proportions in our emotional lives.

### "You'd Better Watch Out"

Soon after birth we learn to expect certain parental reactions when we misbehave. We are told, "Since you did that, you must be punished." Each time we fall short of a parental standard, we learn to expect punishment. We develop a "balanced scale" concept. We think, "When I do wrong, I'll be punished. This makes me anxious and upset. Once my punishment is over, I'm again relieved. I've paid my debts and can operate without fear." The punishment atones for the misdeeds and in that way relieves anxiety.

In spite of our permissive society, most of us continue to harbor some fears of punishment or retribution. No parent goes through life without occasionally losing his temper with his children. And every parent, no matter how cool and collected, occasionally threatens his child with serious consequences for his misbehavior. These threats and angry comments can instill as deep a fear of punishment as actual physical discipline.

When our parents are no longer present to punish our misdeeds, a problem arises: how can this anxiety be alleviated? Years of discipline have taught us, "When you're wrong, you must be punished." Even in our parents' absence this nagging thought persists. To relieve this anxiety, we develop intricate ways of inflicting punishment on ourselves. As children sometimes mimic parents and say, "No, no!" and slap their own wrists, adults also punish and rebuke themselves. A client of mine deliberately cut himself with razor blades as "penance." He felt deep guilt over sexual behavior and the self-inflicted pain gave temporary relief.

According to the church historian Eusebius, the early church father Origen castrated himself so that he could give women religious instruction without temptation! If this report is true, it is another extreme example of self-inflicted punishment because of fear and guilt over sexual impulses.

Most people don't turn to physical forms of punishment. Instead, we substitute a mental pain or threat of punishment. We stab ourselves with: "You misbehaved. You shouldn't act that way. Sometime you're going to get caught and really get it." This sort of threat replaces the punishments we feared as children.

The Ancient Mariner in Coleridge's poem portrays the haunting fear of a guilty man. After cruelly killing the albatross that had brought him safety, he was plagued with fears of punishment and revenge. Coleridge wrote:

> Like one, that on a lonesome road
> Doth walk in fear and dread
> And having once turned round walks on,
> And turns no more his head;
> Because he knows, a frightful fiend
> Doth close behind him tread.

Sometimes we transfer our fear of punishment to God. We feel, "Somehow, somewhere, God is going to get even." We live under constant expectation of judgment for misdeeds. Sometimes we fear God will punish us by involving us in an accident or illness. Many women are afraid they will give birth to a deformed child or experience some unusual suffering. These types of fearful feelings make punishment a relentless companion.

### "Shame, Shame on You"

The second part of guilt-emotion is known to most of us. How many of us have not cringed at the words: "Shame on you; you know better than that"? Or perhaps we were reprimanded even more strongly by parents who said, "Look how you have let us down. After all we've done for you, how could you hurt us this way?" This kind of verbal punishment leads to a basic cause of depression—the loss of self-esteem. By self-esteem we mean our basic evaluation of ourselves—our sense of value and of worth.

If we are given repeated messages that we're "naughty" in our formative years, deep feelings of inadequacy and a poor self-image develop. Even after reaching adulthood, a person with this type of upbringing maintains his poor self-image. He repeatedly feels: "I'm sure to be a failure." In the absence of his parents, his internal corrective-self continues to whisper: "Shame on you. You're a bad person."

One sign of this condition is an inability to relax. Some of us must keep continually busy. We work long hours and take little time for rest and relaxation. We keep saying we need a rest, but when vacations come we soon get edgy. We're not content to "take it easy." The underlying irritant is a sense of guilt. We fear we are not worthy or important if we're not busy. Or worse yet, we unconsciously fear some punishment will come if we don't keep our noses to the grindstone.

In religious homes this pattern is sometimes intensified. The child is taught that he is sinful and deeply deserving of judgment. While true in a very important sense, the misuse of these concepts may cause the child to obey his parents at the expense of his inner feelings of self-respect.

## The Silent Treatment

The third ingredient of the guilt emotion is a fear of rejection and isolation. All children are occasional objects of a loved one's anger. Parents, siblings, friends, or admired teachers may react to our misconduct with anger and frustration. In extreme cases they scream: "I hate you!" or "Get out of my sight!"

Some parents find that withdrawal of love is a quick way to enforce good behavior. Faced with the consequence of losing love, most of us try to change to please the ones we love. To a young child, even the threat of emotional rejection instills a deep fear. He thinks, "When I do wrong, my parents get angry and send me to my room or spank me hard. They don't love me." No matter how many times he's told, "We love you just the way you are," the occasions of parental anger and frustration constantly undermine the message of unconditional love.

The mother of an adopted child told me of the great difficulty she had controlling her new daughter. She tried everything and finally found a way that worked. "I tell her," she said proudly, "God doesn't love you when you're naughty!" The long-range effects of such a threat on an impressionable child could be spiritually crippling.

Each of us is reared by very human parents, and we all have some experiences that suggest: "People love you less when you are naughty." So as adults we suffer feelings of rejection when we fall short of our ideals. Unfortunately, these feelings are often disguised and we fail to recognize their presence.

After several months of counseling, Mary, a thirty-five-year-old woman suffering from depression, was discussing her guilt feelings. She said, "If I want or ask for nice things, I feel guilty. I think I should be satisfied with what I have." To help her understand her conflicts, I asked, "How did you feel when you were a child and your father told you 'No'?" She immediately replied, "I thought I didn't deserve anything." "But how did you feel about your father?" I asked.

"Angry," she replied, "but I couldn't tell him. I was never allowed to be angry with my father." "What would you like to have told him if you hadn't been so afraid?" I asked. "I'd probably have said, 'You don't love me and you don't understand. You don't know how important it is to me. You don't care about me!' "After a moment I said, "What would your dad have done if you told him how you felt?" "I keep thinking he would have hit me across the face—or he might have walked out the door. I don't know—he never hit me— maybe once. Mother said he slapped me, but I don't remember. That's what he did to Mother." Then she broke into tears.

What started as a feeling of guilt reflected by Mary's statement, "I don't deserve anything," had now been revealed as a fear of losing her father's love. Her mental mechanisms had replaced that painful fear with a feeling of guilt which said, "You don't deserve to get what you want." Unpleasant as it was, this feeling was easier to bear than living in dread of her father's disapproval.

So, out of the disciplinary and retaliatory practices of our parents and other influential people we develop: (1) a form of self-punishment that replaces the external punishment received or expected during childhood years; (2) a loss of self-esteem or a feeling of unworthiness; (3) a nagging anxiety over loss of love for misbehavior.

As adults, when we fall short of our ideals, our punitive-self goes into action. It evokes threats of punishment, rejection or loss of self-esteem, the feelings we experience as guilt. Only as we gain insight into how these punitive pressures work can we make lasting progress in overcoming their negative influence and turning our energies to more positive life pursuits.

4

# The Great Guilt Failure

Nobody likes to feel guilty. The misery of conscious guilt and the more subtle stresses of unconscious guilt rob us of happiness, yet the pain causes us to readily inflict guilt on others.

At a social gathering I attended, a wife publicly vented her displeasure that her husband did not spend enough time at home. In front of him she said, "John *never* spends time with the family. I think he loves his work more than us." Obviously, she was trying to make John feel like a rat in front of his friends, hoping he would be shamed into staying home more. Occasionally this works, but more often it only increases the husband's resentment and pushes him to find more escapes from his nagging wife.

Joan, a young housewife who was coming to me for counseling, described a family budget conflict. When her husband found out she had spent three dollars over their clothes allowance for the month, he said in disgust, "You can count on the fact we'll never have anything nice. You refuse to let me balance the budget. You have no common sense."

He succeeded, of course, in making her feel guilty. She thought she'd done a stupid thing, felt depressed, and said she was sorry. But underneath she was hopping mad. She resented his harsh words and inwardly blamed him for being a poor provider.

This often happens when we try to motivate others by guilt. We might produce desired changes, but the consequent guilt feelings usually create more pressures that generate resentment and conflicts that further disrupt relationships.

## Guilt Games

Since we know this sometimes happens, we ought to ask ourselves: Does guilt really work? When we are threatened with rejection, punishment, or loss of self-esteem, do we improve our performance? Or do we just get under a bigger pile? Actually, we usually come up with one of four reactions, none of which is healthy. These reactions are ways of avoiding the pain of guilt and might be called "guilt games."

### Guilt Game One: "I Give Up"

One of the easiest—but most painful—ways to handle guilt feelings is to give up and become depressed. We accept guilt's accusation and feel rotten. When this happens, it becomes very difficult to function properly. The fear of punishment, sense of worthlessness, or feeling of rejection places a heavy burden on our emotional lives and drains us of energy we could otherwise spend on constructive endeavors. People who have surrendered to feelings of guilt and self-deprecia- tion usually become chronically depressed.

### Guilt Game Two: "I'll Show You"

Another common response to guilt motivation is anger and rebellion. We react by thinking: "I'll show you!" For example, when someone implies: "I won't accept you unless you act the way I want," we may feel like retorting, "If you don't like me the way I am, forget it." If someone says, "You sure made a mess out of that, and if you do it again it's going to cost you," we may feel like saying, "Just try to catch me" or "Wait till your back is turned and I'll do what I want."

Many teen-agers feel this way. They obey their parents because of threats of punishment, but at the same time they're thinking, "Just wait till I'm eighteen—then I'll show you!"

Jerry, a minister's son, told me he had always felt "on display." He tried to play the role of "preacher's kid," but felt he could never please his parents or meet their expectations. Gradually he began to get depressed. He condemned himself, felt guilty, and isolated himself from others. Then he began to drink. Recalling one of his drinking sprees, he said, "I lifted a bottle to my mouth and yelled, 'Here's one for the deacon board!'" Obviously, he was rebelling against the church and trying to escape a nagging sense of guilt and failure. He figured he could never please his parents, no matter what he did, so he finally threw it all out.

Many people do the same with God. They try to obey the Bible and Christian standards to the hilt. Finally it becomes too hard and their guilt becomes too great, so they profess to be atheists or agnostics and start "living it up." They figure, "If you can't beat it (sin) you might as well join it."

Others don't rebel so courageously. They take a more passive route. They continue to give verbal assent to the Christian faith but fail to get involved. They are routinely late, constantly preoccupied, or just "not interested." This passive resistance also shows up in married life.

Responding to the threats, naggings, or guilt motivations of a mate, the husband or wife fights back with passivity. He or she fails to get ready on time, lets household tasks go undone, or gets involved in activities that neglect the family. In this way the guilt-ridden person fights back. Unfortunately, this passive rebellion stirs up more anger and guilt and compounds the problem.

What most of us don't realize is that these are normal reactions to guilt feelings. We should realistically expect guilt to stir up rebellion. This is what the New Testament teaches.

Paul wrote, "*And the law came in that the transgression might increase;* but where sin increased, grace abounded all the more" (Romans 5:20, *NASB*). The Amplified Bible translates that verse: "But then law came in, [only] to expand and increase the trespass [making it more apparent and exciting opposition]."

One purpose of the law of Moses with its threats of punishment and associated guilt feelings was to make us sin more! The law is like a "Wet-Paint-Do-Not-Touch" sign. Our immediate response is to want to touch the forbidden spot. God knows we are inwardly rebellious even when we don't recognize it, and the law exposes our rebellion in outward sins. This doesn't mean the law creates something; it seizes the dormant rebellion and drags it into the open so we realize its presence.

Paul gives us a powerful illustration from his own life. He writes:

"What shall we say then? Is the law sin? May it never be! On the contrary, I would not have come to know sin except through the law; for I would not have known about coveting if the law had not said, 'You shall not covet.' But sin, taking opportunity through the commandment, produced in me coveting of every kind; for apart from the law sin is dead. And I was once alive apart from the law; but when the commandment came, sin became alive, and I died; and this commandment, which was to result in life, proved to result in death for me; for sin, taking opportunity through the commandment, deceived me, and through it killed me. So then, the law is holy, and the commandment is holy and righteous and good" (Romans 7:7-12, *NASB*).

Paul became aware of the depth of his own sinfulness through the commandment, "You shall not covet." Though he knew he should obey the commandment, he found himself rebelling against it. The more he knew what he should do, the less he found himself doing it. And the more guilty he became. This experience is common to all of us. Threats of the law and guilty feelings frequently stir up increased rebellion.

### Guilt Game Three: "I'm Not That Bad"

The third basic reaction to guilt feelings is to deny them. We do this by rationalizing away our failures and our sins. We say things like, "Compared to other people, I'm not so bad"—"It really couldn't be helped"—"I did the best I could." Sometimes we deny our faults entirely. We say, "There's nothing wrong with that, that's just the way I am"; or "That's human nature."

Sometimes this reaction includes blaming others. We develop ingenious ways of deceiving ourselves and others with the use of the "I'm-not-that-bad" approach. Consequently we dull our moral perceptions as to what is really right and wrong.

The Bible is filled with illustrations of this guilt reaction. When Adam sinned and God confronted him in the garden, Adam's lame response for plunging the human race into sin was, "The woman whom thou gavest to be with me, she gave me from the tree and I ate" (Genesis 3:12). In other words: "God, the reason I went wrong was Eve; since you gave me Eve, it's all your fault."

Saul, the first king of Israel, was commissioned by the Prophet Samuel to exterminate the corrupt Amalekite civilization. Instead, King Saul preserved the best goods and spared many of the leaders. Listen to what he says when Samuel confronts him over his disobedience: "I did obey the voice of the Lord, and went on the mission on which the Lord sent me. . . . But the people took some of the spoil . . . to sacrifice to the Lord God. . . . (1 Samuel 15:20, 21, *NASB*).

Instead of admitting that he had *not* obeyed God, Saul responds that *the people* were at fault. And even that fault wasn't so bad because they were going to use the loot for religious sacrifice! Saul worked out a neat alibi for his refusal to obey God and simply swept away his conscious guilt feelings.

When Moses led the Israelites out of Egypt into Sinai's wilderness, they went through several harrowing experiences as God tried to teach them to trust him. When they ran out of water the people "grumbled against Moses and said, 'Why, now have you brought us up from Egypt to kill us and our children and our livestock with thirst?'" (Exodus 17:3, *NASB*). Instead of facing up to their own lack of faith and admitting their need to God, they took the easy way out: "There's nothing wrong with us; it's all *Moses'* fault."

Unfortunately, the propensity for blaming others for our faults didn't die with Adam, Saul, or the Israelites. We all do this continually. We argue with our mates, declare our innocence and put the blame on them. We do poorly at school, and blame the professor. And we get fired because "the boss is impossible." Each time we do this, we deny our own responsibilities and failings. This propensity for blaming others relies on the defense mechanisms of rationalization and projection. And instead of resolving our problem, we burrow deeper into a rut of self-deception and character stagnation.

### Guilt Game Four: "I'm Sorry—Please Don't Punish Me"

This final guilt game is the most clever and deceptive of all. When we feel guilty, we feel miserable: we like ourselves less, feel a sense of alienation from God, and fear his punishment or retribution. The guilt becomes so painful that we admit we're wrong to get relief, ask forgiveness, and wait for the pain to go away. Often this confession works like a magic wand—in no time at all the guilt seems to vanish and we feel good about ourselves, accepted by God and free from punishment.

But what was the motive for confession? Were we concerned about the person we hurt? Were we sorry about doing wrong? Or were we just trying to rid ourselves of unpleasant guilt feelings? I think we will have to admit that much of our confession is done more to relieve the pangs of guilt than to alter our behavior for the good of others. Don't we often ask God's forgiveness when we know we will do the same thing again? And aren't our prayers for forgiveness often just a routine, conscience-clearing endeavor?

The Old Testament tells us that one of the Egyptian Pharaohs resorted to this age-old game. When the Israelite slaves pled to emigrate from Egypt, Pharaoh refused. Then God began to work miracles: drinking water turned into blood and plagues of gnats, boils, hail afflicted the nation. A chastened Pharaoh sent to Moses and said, "I have sinned this time; the Lord is the righteous one, and I and my people are the wicked ones. Make supplication to the Lord, for there has been enough of God's thunder and hail; and I will let you go, and you shall stay no longer" (Exodus 9:27, 28, *NASB*).

Sounds genuine, doesn't it? But as soon as the plagues stopped Pharaoh's attitude changed. He wouldn't let the Israelites go. He hadn't really repented; he just wanted relief. Like so many who get caught, he was sorry—but not over his misdeeds. He was sorry about the painful consequences of his misbehavior.

This kind of confession is based on a carryover from our childhood. As children we often said, "I'm sorry" just because we had been caught. As adults, we do a similar thing with God. Since we fear punishment, we quickly say, "I'm sorry." But our confession is much like a child caught with his hand in the cookie jar! We don't want God to "spank" us, so we say we're sorry.

Or perhaps we feel so depressed and sinful that we cannot sleep. To clear our conscience, we confess our faults. Feeling relieved, we go to sleep. But we have not really changed our minds, and the next day our lives will be no different.

## Guilt's Total Failure

All of this leads us to a solid conclusion—guilt doesn't work. The chart illustrates this point. We are all naturally sinful and imperfect. This leads us to wrong thoughts and actions. Then our rebellious actions trigger a fear of punishment, a lowered self-evaluation, or a fear of rejection. In response to this we either (1) give in and suffer depression and feelings of worthlessness, (2) rebel and fight back by committing even more wrongs, (3) deny we did any wrong at all and put the blame on someone else, or (4) superficially acknowledge our faults to get rid of the pain, but feel no rightly-motivated desire to change.

None of these reactions promotes our growth. In fact, they make matters worse. No wonder the emphasis on guilt motivation by some churches has turned many away. And no wonder that many who continue to attend church struggle under an oppressive load of self-hate and condemnation.

## Does the Bible Promote Guilt?

If guilt is so bad, what does the Bible have to say about it? Most people assume that the Bible teaches us to feel guilty. Yet why would a loving and wise God promote such an unhealthy, destructive emotion? The answer to this dilemma lies in a proper understanding of the biblical use of guilt.

*Civil guilt* or legal guilt is the violation of human law. When we exceed the speed limit, for example, we are guilty of breaking the law. We may not feel guilty, but that makes no difference. Civil guilt is an objective fact; it is not a feeling.

*Theological guilt* is the violation of divine law. Like civil guilt, this is an objective fact. Regardless of what we feel, the Bible teaches that we are all imperfect and sinful. Because of this, we break God's moral laws in thought, word, and action. Isaiah says, "All of us like sheep have gone astray. Each of us has turned to his own way" (53:6, *NASB*). Although we may not feel this estrangement consciously, the Bible says this is our natural condition. We are guilty before God.

*Psychological guilt* is what we have talked about so far in this book. It is a *feeling*. It is the painful realization, "I have failed; I should have done better." As we have shown, we may have civil and theological guilt without feeling psychologically guilty, or we may be legally innocent and continue to feel guilty over nothing.

*Constructive sorrow* is discussed in the Bible in 2 Corinthians 7:9-10 and other places. This differs from ordinary psychological guilt so greatly that we prefer not to attach

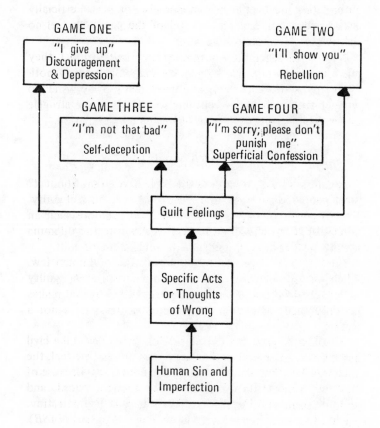

the name "guilt" to it at all, though we list it here. It is the only reaction to wrongdoing that produces lasting change for the right reasons. It does not involve the use of guilt games and does not involve the feelings of self-condemnation of psychological guilt. We will discuss it at length later in this book. Some prefer to call constructive sorrow "true guilt" as distinguished from "false guilt." We think this confuses the issue. It's more helpful to consider the damaging psychological guilt in one category and constructive sorrow in another.

When we come to the Bible we find an interesting paradox. Although the Bible discusses legal guilt and theological guilt, it never tells the Christian to feel psychological guilt.

James 2:10, for example, states: "For whoever keeps the whole law, yet stumbles in one point, he has become guilty of all" (*NASB*). Jesus says in the sermon on the mount: "Whoever shall say, 'You fool,' shall be guilty enough to go into the hell of fire" (Matthew 5:22, *NASB*). These and other passages demonstrate that God holds man accountable for violation of divine law, and that he is *theologically* guilty.

*But not once does the Bible encourage believers in Jesus Christ to accept psychological guilt. Not once are Christians commanded to have a fear of punishment, a sense of worthlessness, or a feeling of rejection.* It's significant to note that of the three New Testament Greek words translated "guilt" in our language (*hupodikos, opheilo,* and *enochos*), not one of them refers to the *feeling* of guilt. Instead, they mean "to be liable to judgment," "to be guilty of an offense," or "to owe or be indebted to."

In the Christian's life, feelings of psychological guilt are always destructive. This guilt is one of the major causes of spiritual deadness and defeat. In a sincere desire to help people break from their hang-ups, our guilt-inducing statements often press them deeper into wrong or self-deception. The only time guilt serves any useful purpose is in the life of the non-Christian. For him, guilt accentuates his frustrations where he sees his inability to earn God's acceptance on the basis of his efforts. This guilt drives him to seek God's unconditional acceptance through Christ.

At first glance, this view may seem incredibly far out. Most of us have been brought up on a steady diet of guilt. We are told it is God who makes us feel guilty. And we have all felt deeply guilty. To suggest such guilt is not from God seems foreign and unspiritual. Yet we are convinced that Christians have thus welcomed guilt as a wolf in sheep's clothing—and we need to be freed.

Instead of creating psychological guilt, the Bible offers the ultimate resolution of the human guilt dilemma—in the life, death, and resurrection of Jesus Christ. Properly comprehended and applied, the Bible has a perfect plan of guilt reduction. It speaks to each aspect of the guilt-emotion. And it offers a psychologically healthy alternative—constructive sorrow.

In the next four chapters we will take a closer look at the basis for guilt-free living. Chapters Five and Six will lay a foundation for a healthy self-esteem. And Chapters Seven and Eight will show how we can be freed from the fears of punishment and rejection and maintain an unbroken fellowship with our Creator.

5

# Who Am I, Really?

Part way through a counseling hour, I asked a woman named Carol to finish the sentence, "I am . . . " ten times. Thoughtfully she replied:

"I am . . . a poor mother."

"I am . . . a disappointment to my parents."

"I am . . . overweight."

"I am . . . unhappy."

"I am . . . divorced."

She went on to list ten negative things about herself. "I didn't ask you to list ten bad things about yourself," I said encouragingly. "Try again. And this time finish it with good things about yourself."

"No," she said, "I can't."

"Sure you can," I reassured.

"No, I can't," she said tearfully. Finally she managed to say, "I try to be a good mother." And with more encouragement she said, "I try to keep a clean house." This was all the good she could say about herself. And even that was qualified. When she said, "I try," she was indicating she really thought she failed.

Like many, Carol had an extremely poor self-image. She felt bad about herself and could think of few if any positive self-evaluations. Needless to say, she was very unhappy and suffering from intense guilt and depression. To become a happy, well-adjusted person, she would have to develop more positive attitudes toward herself.

All of us have an image of ourselves. We may think of ourselves as very likeable and worthy, or we may have negative self-evaluations and rarely feel happy with ourselves. Most of us are somewhere in between. Psychologists have ascertained that this basic set of attitudes toward ourselves plays a key role in the emotions we call guilt. Accompanying all feelings of guilt is the conscious thought, "I am bad; I should be better." Because of this, it's impossible to separate guilt from lowered self-esteem. In seeking release from guilt, we must take a close look at the matter of self-esteem.

## The Roots of Self-Esteem

*Draw a tree with roots & fruits of Self Esteem*

Like most personality characteristics, our self-image has its roots in early life. If we are given positive feedback from parents, friends, and other people close to us, we will develop a largely positive self-evaluation. But when key people regularly give us negative vibrations, we incorporate these *negative vibes* evaluations into our self-concept and learn to dislike ourselves. By our adolescent years, these attitudes are strongly built into our personalities and become extremely difficult to change.

But while the roots of our self-esteem are firmly established in early childhood, our later life experiences continue to affect our feelings toward ourselves. If our mates and friends encourage us and build us up, we feel an extra bit of self-esteem. If we live with constant criticism, our self-images take a beating. Similarly, our life philosophy and religious view also affect our self concept. Some of us embrace a social or religious atmosphere that encourages growth, esteem, and flexibility. Others are caught in a web of influences that unknowingly tie us down and frustrate personal growth. Let's take a look at two common systems that affect our self-image.

### I'm a Perfect, Unlimited Seagull"

One widely held optimistic view of man has recently gained great popularity through Richard Bach's best-selling *Jonathan Livingston Seagull.* In Bach's book Jonathan is a seagull who refuses to be content with the mundane affairs of life. While other gulls are living routine existences, Jonathan embarks on a self-improvement program. As he gradually perfects his flying technique, he realizes, "We can lift ourselves out of ignorance, we can find ourselves as creatures of excellence and intelligence and skill. We can be free! We can learn to fly."[1]

After even more self-improvement, Jonathan reaches "heaven" and finds he has no limits. Perfection is within reach if he will only realize his full potential. At one point Jonathan tells his friend, Fletcher, "to keep finding yourself, a little more each day, that real, unlimited Fletcher Seagull."[2]

Bach's book is dedicated "to the real Jonathan Seagull who lives within us all." Through this parable he teaches (1) there is no personal God, (2) we are all "sons of God," (3) there are many enlightened spiritual teachers (none of them entirely divine) and (4) all apparent limitations of human nature are just illusions of the mind! We can all move higher and higher, and a "new age" lies ahead if we only realize our full potential. This story is so appealing that over six million copies are now in print.

### If We're So Good—Why All the Problems?

Many psychologists and educators share a similarly optimistic view of man. They believe all men are basically good and that we only need to accept our goodness and realize or "actualize" our full potential. They see this as the basis for a good self-image. In this vein, well-known psychologist Abraham Maslow wrote:

> This inner nature, as much as we know of it so far, seems not to be intrinsically evil but rather neutral or

> positively "good." . . . Since this inner nature is good
> or neutral rather than bad, it is best to bring it out
> and to encourage it rather than to suppress it. If it is
> permitted to guide our life, we grow healthy, fruit-
> ful, and happy.[3]

This sounds great at first. Wouldn't we all like to believe
we are essentially good and only need to be encouraged to
"be ourselves"? And wouldn't we like to think we have no
limitations and could become "perfect unlimited gulls"? The
problem is that this view doesn't square with reality. The
basic dilemmas of our century—war, pollution, government
corruption, economic instability, poverty, prejudice—all are
of human origin. If we are so good, or if we are so capable of
achieving our own perfection, why, after thousands of years,
do we continue to cause and multiply such gigantic problems? Even Maslow, with all his optimism, is forced to
acknowledge this weakness.

> There are certainly good and strong and successful
> men in the world. . . . But it also remains true that
> there are so few of them, even though there *could* be
> so many more, and that they are often badly treated
> by their fellows. So this, too, must be studied, this
> fear of human goodness and greatness, this lack of
> knowledge of how to be good and strong, this inabili-
> ty to turn one's anger into productive activities, this
> fear of maturing, this fear of feeling virtuous, self-
> loving, love-worthy, respect-worthy. Especially must
> we learn how to transcend our foolish tendency to
> let our compassion for the weak generate hatred for
> the strong.[4]

### Building Hope on Quicksand

The optimistic view also has another problem. It is self-
contradictory. It is totally inconsistent with the foundation
on which it's built. Most people who hold this view either
believe a personal God does not exist or that we can't know
anything about him if he does. They believe that man is the
accidental product of time plus chance through evolution.

We are supposedly the most recent animal link in the evolutionary chain. Accordingly, we have no soul, no spirit, and no image of God. We cannot be distinguished from the animal world except on a pragmatic basis, so we have no meaningful origin, no present purpose, and no important end. With these underlying beliefs, an enthusiastic endorsement of human nature is highly illogical. How can we have a high sense of value and of dignity if we are chance happenings on a planet without purpose?

More than fifty years ago philosopher-mathematician Bertrand Russell—who held this humanistic view—penned this eloquent statement of its implications:

> That man is the product of causes which had no prevision of the end they were achieving; that his origin, his growth, his hopes and fears, his loves and his beliefs, are but the outcome of accidental collocations of atoms; that no fire, no heroism, no intensity of thought and feeling can preserve an individual life beyond the grave; that all the labor of all the ages, all the devotion, all the noonday brightness of human genius are destined to extinction in the vast death of the solar system, and that the whole temple of man's achievement must inevitably be buried beneath the debris of a universe in ruins—all these things, if not quite beyond dispute, are yet so nearly certain that no philosophy which rejects them can hope to stand. Only within the scaffolding of these truths, only on the firm foundation of unyielding despair can the soul's habitation henceforth be safely built![5]

Read what he says again: "Only on the firm foundation of unyielding despair can the soul's habitation henceforth be safely built." Such a view consigns us directly to the ash heap! We have no special beginning and no special end. We are indistinct from other forms of life. Our behavior is meaningless, and attempting to alter it is pointless in the long run. If this is true, how can we have any self-esteem? If we are only hunks of matter, how can we have a sense of self-respect and dignity? In spite of well-meaning efforts, this philosophy sinks rapidly in the quicksand of reality.

### "I'm a Lowly, Wretched Worm"

Some churches and religious groups go to the opposite extreme. Instead of emphasizing man's goodness, they focus excessively on his badness. They often gravitate to poetry and hymns with a negative emphasis. Lucy A. Bennett put it this way:

> Though I be nothing, I exult
> In thy divine perfection
> And taste the deep, mysterious joy
> Of absolute subjection.
>
> Though I be nothing, I rejoice
> To find my all in thee:
> Not I, but Christ, forevermore
> Amen! So let it be![6]

Most of us are familiar with John Newton's song:

> Amazing grace, how sweet the sound
> That saved a *wretch like me!*
> I once was lost, but now am found,
> Was blind, but now I see.

Isaac Watts wrote:

> Alas, and did my Saviour bleed
> And did my sovereign die
> Would he devote that sacred head
> *For such a worm as I.*

The common thread running through these verses is a sense of self-abasement. We are either "nothing," "worms," or "wretches." When such graphic words are added to guilt-producing sermons and the usual failures of everyday life, you have a formula for real self-hate! This is especially true for people with poor self-images. Many people believe this negative view is the Bible's exclusive emphasis. This became crystal clear to me when I assigned some graduate students in a theology course to write a paper on, "The Nobility of Man According to the Bible." Several of them told me that they were unaware the Bible said anything about man being noble.

Newton and Watts, of course, had understandable reasons for their despairing view of themselves. John Newton lived a debauched life as a slave trader until he found God, and he felt he'd been a wretch. Isaac Watts lived in a time when theologians emphasized the vast gulf between man and God. Both of these men were great Christians and went on to write many beautiful and inspiring thoughts about God and man. Newton, for example, wrote:

> When we've been there ten thousand years,
> Bright shining as the sun,
> We've no less days to sing God's praise
> Than when we've first begun.

*[handwritten: Reinforces neg. Self image]*

The problem arises when sensitive people pick out these negative, pessimistic statements and use them to reinforce their poor self-images. While these verses picture a certain portion of biblical truth, they do not give a balanced view of God's estimate of man.

*[handwritten: Seagulls or Worms which?]*

## "Who Am I, Really?"

If we're neither a "seagull" nor a "worm," what are we? Anticipating the kernels of truth found in other views, the Bible balances them by declaring we are (1) very special, (2) deeply fallen and (3) greatly loved.

### "I Am Very Special"

*[handwritten: Special Creation]*

The opening pages of Genesis present man in his grandeur. God created us and exalted us above all other created beings. Adam, the first man, was a sin-free, corruption-free, death-free being. God placed him not in a primitive, barren cave but in a home suited to his nature—the beautiful Garden of Eden. He was the capstone of God's creation. He alone of all the living beings was created "in the image of God." And he alone was given dominion over all the earth.

Special – on his change

Genesis 1:26-27 (*NASB*) says: "Then God said, 'Let us make man in our image, according to our likeness; and let them rule over the fish of the sea and over the birds of the sky and over the cattle and over all the earth, and over every creeping thing that creeps on the earth.' And God created man in his own image, in the image of God he created him; male and female he created them." Thus the Bible describes us as originally planned, expressly purposeful, highly significant, and eternally valuable.

"That's fine," you say, "but what about now? Didn't Adam's and Eve's sins obliterate all that?"

Nothing could be further from the truth! Adam did rebel and plunge the human race into sin. And our own rebellion has deeply tarnished the beauty of God's image in us. But we did not suddenly become "non-man." The huge gap between us and the highest animal remains, the image of God remains, and our innate dignity and personal worth remain. They all are marred but they continue to exist.

emphasis on soul

Jesus placed great worth on us. At one point he said our human life is worth more than wealth and possessions of the entire world. He asserted the immeasurable value of a person by asking: "What does it profit a man to gain the whole world and forfeit his soul?" (Mark 8:36, *NASB*).

good

At another time Jesus elevated human life far above plant and animal life. He said if God clothes the wild flowers of the Galilean hillsides so beautifully, "will he not much more do so for you, O men of little faith?" (Matthew 6:30, *NASB).* And he rebuked the religious leaders for not discerning "how much more value is a man than a sheep" (Matthew 12:12, *NASB).*

Writing to the Christians at Corinth, who still reflected their corrupt background, Paul said they bore the stamp of the "image and glory of God" (1 Corinthians 11:7, *NASB*). And James warns us not to curse other men since they retain "the likeness of God" (James 3:9, *NASB*).

The Bible says humans are unbelievably important—we are at the center of God's created universe. Our importance becomes even more incalculable in the light of God's magnificent redemptive plan. Lamenting our plunge into sin, God reached down to rescue us and restore us to himself. Christ didn't die for the animals. And he didn't suffer on the cross because he was obliged to. He gave his life for us because we are so valuable to him! That is why Peter said, "You were not redeemed with perishable things like silver or gold . . . but with . . . the precious blood of Christ" (1 Peter 1:18, 19, *NASB*). Paul also exhorted the Corinthians to serve God because they were "bought with a price" (1 Corinthians 6:20), and he warned the Roman Christians they must set a high example lest they "cause the ruin of one for whom Christ died" (Romans 14:15, *RSV*).

This biblical teaching of the dignity and value of man has been an untold and often unrecognized blessing to the world. Christianity was born into an age when human life was cheap. Blood was spilled without remorse. The aged, the sick, and even the infant were readily expendable. As the influence of Christianity expanded, it began to revolutionize the ancient world's view of man. Historian R. R. Palmer describes the impact:

> It is impossible to exaggerate the importance of the coming of Christianity. It brought with it . . . an altogether new sense of human life. Where the Greeks had shown man his mind, the Christians showed him his soul; and they taught that in the sight of God all souls were equal, and that every human life was sacrosanct and inviolate. . . . Where the Greeks had identified the beautiful and the good, had thought ugliness to be bad, and had shrunk from disease and imperfection and from everything misshapen as horrible and repulsive, the Christians . . . sought out the diseased, the crippled, and the mutilated to give them help. Love, for the ancients, was never quite distinguished from Venus; for the Christians, who held that God was love, it took on deep overtones of sacrifice and compassion.[7]

But the dignity and worth of man are only one side of the coin. The Bible also portrays us as rebellious creatures.

## "I am Deeply Fallen"

Genesis frankly records man's first rebellion against God. It also shows the results of that rebellion in our alienation from God, ourselves, and others. The evidence of this alienation is widespread in our world today, and it's no use to try to whitewash the biblical picture of the depths of human sin. Consider these divine evaluations of our condition.

"God has looked down from heaven upon the sons of men, to see if there is anyone who understands, who seeks after God. Everyone of them has turned aside; together they have become corrupt; there is no one who does good, not even one" (Psalm 53:2, 3, *NASB*).

"The heart is more deceitful than all else and is desperately sick; who can understand it?" (Jeremiah 17:9, *NASB*).

"All have sinned and fall short of the glory of God" (Romans 3:23, *RSV*).

"If we say that we have no sin, we are deceiving ourselves and the truth is not in us" (1 John 1:8, *NASB*).

When the Bible mentions sin, it usually means "to miss the mark." The Old Testament book of Judges describes some Hebrew warriors with sling shots "who could sling a stone at a hair and not miss." The word for "miss" is the Hebrew word *chatah*—usually translated "to sin." Paul explains the concept further in Romans, where he says, "All have sinned and fall short of the glory of God." Here he connects sin with failing to attain God's moral glory and perfection. The Westminster Confession says, "Sin is any want of conformity unto, or transgression of, the law of God." In God's estimate, we are likened to a marksman who never hits the bulls eye, or the marathon runner who must go twenty-six miles but only makes ten. And the target or goal isn't the shifting mark set by our society, it's the perfect standard of a loving God.

Theologians sometimes use the word "depravity" to describe our condition. Taking biblical statements like "All have sinned" and "There is none righteous," they have built a concept known as "total depravity." Popularized by followers of John Calvin, this refers to the extent of human sinfulness and rebellion. Unfortunately, it is usually misunderstood.

Think about your own concept of depravity. What is your mental picture of a "depraved person"? Was it the traditional "bum on skid row?" An unkempt, sloppily dressed, unshaven drunk; or did you envision a murderer, a drug-crazed addict, or a sex fiend? For most people, this is the image conjured up by the term "total depravity."

Now envision a gathering of some of the world's great Christian leaders, such as the Apostle Paul, John Wesley, Billy Graham and a few other "spiritual giants." Imagine them in a deeply spiritual discussion—now think "depravity"; the bible says these men also are totally depraved!

Theologically, depravity means that God has a perfect standard of what we ought to be, and we never do *anything* that reaches this standard, even in our best moments. Jesus said in the sermon on the mount, "Therefore, you are to be perfect, as your heavenly Father is perfect" (Matthew 5:48, *NASB*), yet no man, by himself, has been perfect in anything. No matter how noble an act we perform, it is tainted with some degree of selfishness or induced by a wrong motive, or it is never as complete as it should be. Our constant tendency to assert our own will over God's distorts to some degree every area of our life.

Unfortunately, many people think depravity means we are devoid of any good attributes according to human standards. They think we are without any conscience or impulse to do good. And they think "except for the grace of God" we would all be like the "skid row bum." This is far from true. Even without the direct influence of the Holy Spirit, many of us would be upstanding citizens—but destined for eternal separation from God because we fail to meet his perfect requirements.

It helps to understand the difference between "worth" and "value" on the one hand and "righteousness" and "holiness" on the other. While we all fall short of God's standards, we are still of immense value and worth to God. We are so valuable, in fact, that Christ paid the ultimate price to restore us to fellowship with God. Even though we are *unrighteous,* we are immensely *valuable* to God. Even though we are *depraved* (in the sense we have described), we still have great worth.

This biblical insight on depravity gives us a realistic approach to life. It explains what is wrong with the world, and with each one of us. Yet it also gives us an unshakable basis for positive self-esteem.

### *"I Am Loved"*

Fortunately, depravity is only part of the story. The depth of our sinfulness summoned the boundless love of God. He gave his very best—Christ—for us at our very worst. Paul made this clear when he wrote, "But God demonstrates his own love toward us, in that while we were yet sinners, Christ died for us" (Romans 5:8, *NASB*).

In an even more startling expression of God's unfathomable love for us, the Apostle John records a prayer of Christ shortly before his crucifixion. Christ prayed about the people who would place their confidence in him and asked God to make it clear that he loves us just as he loves Christ.

"Neither for these alone do I pray—it is not for their sake only that I make this request—but also for all those who will ever come to believe (trust, cling to, rely on) me through their word and teaching; so that they all may be one [just] as you, Father, are in me and I in you, that they also may be one in us, so that the world may believe and be convinced that you have sent me. I have given to them the glory and honor which you have given me, that they may be one, [even] as we are one: I in them and you in me, in order that they may become one and perfectly united, that the world may know and [definitely] recognize that you sent me, and that you have loved them [even] as you have loved me" (John 17:20-23, *Amp.*).

Here Christ says he not only passes on to us the glory given him by God, but that God the Father loves us with the same love he loves his Son! What a deep sense of self-esteem this should impart. We are loved by God with the identical love he gave his Son! This, as much as any other fact, should cancel out self-hatred. If God, our creator and the highest moral authority in the universe, loves us—we shouldn't contradict him and tell him he's making a grave mistake!

Yet on the emotional level many of us find it hard to accept and feel such love toward ourselves. One of the reasons is our habit of making love conditional.

Don't we choose our friends and even our marriage partners after making evaluations of their worth to us? If someone is attractive, intelligent, friendly, or athletic, we are likely to show strong interest in him. Similarly, when we succeed or win some special honor, we receive increased interest from other people. Years of this sort of experience make us feel we are loved when we perform acceptably or impressively. When we don't, we feel less important and less lovable.

Unfortunately, this gets the self-image cart before the horse and we go nowhere. Good performance may flow from a person striving for approval but even then he won't feel accepted. But a person with a high level of self-acceptance will produce good results naturally and contentedly.

In human relationships, probably the strongest experience of acceptance that isn't based on performance is felt between a parent and child. Especially when children are small, they do little to earn parental love. In fact, they sometimes do the opposite. They cry in the middle of the night, throw tantrums, and cause all sorts of inconvenience. When they are a little older, they want their Cheerios at 6:30 in the morning even though we're sick in bed, and they continue to make "unreasonable demands." Despite these frustrations, most of us deeply love our little children. We will sacrifice almost anything for their welfare, just because of who they are—they are our children and that is reason enough to love them.

This pictures the way God looks at us. Though we're often selfish and rebellious, he loves us just the same. He is totally devoted to our welfare, just because we are his children. We should see ourselves as he does. Even when we're bad, we should remember our unconditional value. A Godlike respect for ourselves should be at the core of our self-image. We should see ourselves as important children of God, valuable just for who we are.

FOOTNOTES

1. Bach, Richard, *Jonathan Livingston Seagull* (New York: Macmillan, 1970), p. 30.

2. *Ibid.,* pp. 124, 125.

3. Maslow, Abraham, *Toward a Psychology of Being* (New York: D. Van Nostrand Reinhold Co., Inc., 1968) p. 4.

4. Maslow, *ibid.,* p. iv.

5. Russell, Bertrand, *A Free Man's Worship,* in P. Edwards (ed.), *Why I Am Not A Christian* and other essays on religion and related subjects (New York: Simon and Schuster, 1956) p. 107.

6. Quoted in *Born Crucified,* by L. E. Maxwell (Chicago: Moody Press, 1945) p. 60.

7. Palmer, R. R., *A History of the Modern World* (New York: Alfred A. Knopf, 1953) p. 11.

# The Liberated Self

Recently I heard a young man named John sing an inspiring solo at a Sunday morning church service. Afterward, when someone remarked how beautifully it was sung and how it encouraged and helped him, John replied, "I didn't do it; it was God."

Behind these words lies a problem we all face. The Bible says we are sinful and imperfect. It also says God is perfect. The conclusion many draw from this is that anything that's good must come from God, and anything that's bad comes from us. But wait a minute! Who was really singing? Wasn't it John's voice? Hadn't he sacrificed hours of spare time to develop his vocal talent? And if he hadn't showed up, there would have been no solo.

## The Identity Crisis

This poses some important questions. Where is the merger of human and divine endeavor? At what point does God end and we begin? What can we expect from God and what should we expect from ourselves? If we "deny" or "crucify" ourselves, is God then free to work through us? Or if we express our own uniqueness, do we "hinder" and "quench" his work? The answer to these questions comes from an understanding of four New Testament words used to describe various aspects of our personalities.

### The Ego: the Total You

The Greek word Paul used for "I" is "*ego.*" By it, he means the total person or the self. Although the Bible uses words like spirit, soul, and heart to describe limited aspects of our personalities, it uses self or ego to encompass the whole man. Similarly, when it says, "you," it means the totality of our being.

### The "Flesh": the Real Culprit

Put three drops of ink in a glass of water and soon all of the water is discolored. The ink is not the *same* as the water, but it permeates and affects it all. In the same way, the Bible says our whole self is influenced by sin. We are permeated throughout by imperfection and a tendency to rebel. This sinfulness affects our entire lives. It reaches our minds, our feelings, our bodies, and our wills. Like the ink in water, it touches our whole being, but is not identical to it.

In speaking of this fallenness or sinfulness, the Bible often uses the term "*flesh.*" For example, Paul says, "Now the deeds of the flesh are evident, which are: immorality, impurity, sensuality, . . . strife, jealousy, outbursts of anger . . . " (Galatians 5:19-21, *NASB*). The flesh here does not refer to our material flesh and bones. It refers instead to the sin-principle in us all—the "ink" that permeates our total being.

Sometimes the Bible uses the word "sin" to mean the same as "flesh." First John 1:8 says, "If we say that we have no sin, we are deceiving ourselves and the truth is not in us" (*NASB*). Here again, "sin" isn't some specific act or thought of sin. Instead, it's the inner principle of rebellion that influences our total lives.

Since the biblical "flesh" is the tendency of our whole person toward sin and in opposition to God, we are warned not to respond to "the desires of the flesh" (Galatians 5:16,

*NASB*). Paul referred to this principle when he said, "For I know that in me (that is, in my flesh) dwells no good thing" (Romans 7:18). Paul wasn't saying his body was bad and that physical pleasures were sinful. Instead, he was saying that in the sin-principle—in that selfish, rebellious force—there is nothing good.

### Don't Confuse These Two!

"Ego" or "self" must not be confused with "flesh." Ego is our whole being. Flesh is the "fallenness" in us. This distinction is frequently apparent in the Bible. For example, in Romans 7:17 Paul says: "So no longer am I [ego] the one doing it, but sin [my fallenness] which dwells in me [ego]" (paraphrased). Here the flesh appears as a force within the ego, but *not the same* as the ego. Similarly, in Romans 6:11 Paul says, "Reckon yourself [ego] dead to sin [your fallenness], but alive to God" (paraphrased). Commonly this passage is misinterpreted to mean, "Be dead to yourself." Actually, it says the self is to be dead to sin and very much alive to God. The self is to be alive, prosperous, and growing. For the regenerated self is going to spend eternity with God.

### The "Old Man": Who You Used To Be

Another important biblical term is "the old man." Paul says in Romans 6:6 that we are to know "that our old self was crucified with him, that our body of sin might be done away with, that we should no longer be slaves to sin" (*NASB*). Similarly in Colossians 3:9 and Ephesians 4:22-24 Christians are described as those who have "put off" the "old man."

The "old man" is often made synonymous with the "flesh." But a careful study of the Bible reveals that the "old man" is probably not the same. The *flesh* is an irrational force. The *old man* is a person, a whole being. The *old man* describes us when we were not believers—before we met Christ. It describes us as apart from Christ, unforgiven, alienated, and totally subject to our own fallenness. In contrast, as believers, we are now called "new men." The "old man" has passed out of existence. We now exist as new people in a new relationship. We are so different that God considers us "new beings."[1]

Suppose you were once a citizen of a foreign country. Then you came to the United States and took out a new citizenship with all its rights and privileges. The former citizen, belonging to the old country, no longer exists in that relationship. As a person you still have old habits, memories, and patterns, but your life is greatly changed and your relationship is very different because you are now a United States citizen. Your former relationship to your old country is broken and you are considered a "new man."

### The "New Man": Who You Are Now

When we believe in Jesus Christ, our self is not suddenly replaced with a new and sinless being. But an incredible change does occur. This change is so revolutionary that Jesus describes it as being "born again" (John 3:5-7).

Paul says we become new people. He writes, "If anyone is in Christ he is a *new creation;* the old has passed away, behold, the new has come" (2 Corinthians 5:17, *RSV*). Paul says the self—the entire personality—is so changed and renewed that the whole man is seen as a new creation.

While the mechanics of this renewal are invisible and mysterious, its effects are great. We suddenly become alive and responsive to God and receive the potential for overcoming much of our rebellion. Although many old habits and problems from "the old country" continue to exist, we have a new desire to serve and follow God.

### Your Personal Civil War

This radical change also brings about a new conflict. There are now two opposing principles in our personalities. On the one hand, we have a desire for God, righteousness, and love. On the other, we have a pull toward self-centeredness, pride, and rebellion. The desire for God has its source in God's original creation of man in his image and in the new life-principle that came into us when we became Christians. The pull toward self-centeredness continues from the fallenness or sin-principle which remains within us even after we become new men. Joining in this battle is the Holy Spirit pulling us toward the good and the devil pulling us toward the bad. Paul graphically portrays this struggle:

"The law is good, then, and the trouble is not there but with me, because I am sold into slavery with sin as my owner. I don't understand myself at all, for I really want to do what is right, but I can't. I do what I don't want to—what I hate. I know perfectly well that what I am doing is wrong, and my bad conscience proves that I agree with these laws I am breaking. But I can't help myself, because I'm no longer doing it. It is sin inside me that is stronger than I am that makes me do these evil things.

"I know I am rotten through and through so far as my old sinful nature is concerned. No matter which way I turn I can't make myself do right. I want to but I can't. When I want to do good, I don't; and when I try not to do wrong, I do it anyway. Now if I am doing what I don't want to, it is plain where the trouble is: sin still has me in its evil grasp.

"It seems to be a fact of life that when I want to do what is right, I inevitably do what is wrong. I love to do God's will so far as my new nature is concerned; but there is something else deep within me, in my lower nature, that is at war with my mind and wins the fight and makes me a slave to the sin that is still within me. In my mind I want to be God's willing servant but instead I find myself still enslaved to sin.

"So you see how it is: my new life tells me to do right, but the old nature that is still inside me loves to sin. Oh, what a terrible predicament I'm in! Who will free me from my slavery to this deadly lower nature? Thank God! It has been done by Jesus Christ our Lord. He has set me free" (Romans 7:14-25, *TLB*).

As a new man in Christ, Paul's deepest desire was to serve God. He said, "I agree with the law and I know it's good." In the depths of his personality he really wanted to do right. But his fallenness impeded his progress. From the very moment of his birth he had been operating on the basis of a sin-dominated, self-seeking principle. All the longstanding habits and rebellious attitudes of that principle remained, struggling against the new. This caused a split in Paul. Part of him was striving for the good while his fallenness was struggling against it. How do we solve this difficult dilemma?

## Self-Denial That Isn't

Some people want to solve it through what they call self-denial. They say we should "crucify" or "deny" ourselves in order to get out of God's way. People who carry this to extremes sometimes develop a set of "disciplines" to promote this self-purging process. This approach was especially popular a few hundred years after Christianity started. It got so far out that a group arose called the "pole-sitting saints." They tried to purify their souls by isolating themselves from the world on small platforms atop high poles! Paul tells us that such an approach will never work. He says, "These are matters which have, to be sure, the appearance of wisdom in self-made religion and self-abasement and severe treatment of the body, but are of no value against fleshly indulgence" (Colossians 2:23, *NASB*).

Contemporary writers on Christian living would never advocate such ridiculous extremes, yet they make statements which can lead to the same kind of self-abasement. Consider this quote in a 1971 book: "Self—the old sin nature—is also the object of his [God's] abhorrence and he yearns to rid us of its control and dominion by putting it to the cross of Christ."[2]

The problem with this approach is that it confuses the *self* with the *flesh*. This encourages self-punishment to "get rid of" the flesh. Although the writer quoted above may have meant God hates the "flesh," his choice of the word "self" is confusing and readily promotes neurotic self-hatred.

What we should be calling for is death to our *fallenness* and *sinfulness*, but not death to the *self*. Those who are overly sensitive and prone to depression immediately pick up these teachings. Thinking God wants them to hate themselves, they attempt to endure life as a kind of experiential suicide.

### Self-Denial That Is

True self-denial is quite different. Jesus said, "If anyone wants to be a follower of mine, let him *deny himself* and take up his cross and follow me" (Matthew 16:24, *TLB*). By self-denial he meant that we should be willing to deny ourselves certain pleasures and desires to accomplish higher and more important purposes. This kind of self-denial is never an end in itself; it is always tied to a worthy goal.

*Sometimes we are called on to deny ourselves physical or financial possessions so that we can share with those who are more needy.* Jesus said, "If you have two coats . . . give one to the poor. If you have extra food, give it away to those who are hungry" (Luke 3:11, *TLB*).

*Sometimes we must deny ourselves some pleasures in order not to offend others or put a roadblock in their path.* Paul said he wouldn't eat meat that had been offered to idols if it would cause a Christian brother to sin, and he challenges us to "determine this—not to put an obstacle or a stumbling block in a brother's way" (Romans 14:13, *NASB*).

*The Bible also tells us to deny or crucify our fallenness.* Paul, for example, writes: "Therefore do not let sin reign in your mortal body, that you should obey its lusts, and do not go on presenting the members of your body to sin as instruments of unrighteousness; but present yourselves to God as those alive from the dead, and your members as instruments of righteousness to God" (Romans 6:12, 13, *NASB*).

Peter wrote, "Dear brothers, you are only visitors here. Since your real home is in heaven I beg you to keep away from the evil pleasures of this world; they are not for you, for they fight against your very souls" (1 Peter 2:11, *TLB*).

In these passages we are not told to deny or crucify our ego; instead, we are told to deny expression to our fallenness because it opposes our personal growth and happiness.

*Another reason for self-denial is to help spread the Christian message.* Paul gave up his life for this goal. We cannot make everything pleasureful and easy if we are going to accomplish anything significant. The accomplished musician, the star athlete, the wise mother, and the skilled craftsman must all sacrifice some things to develop their skills for their main mission in life. But this kind of self-denial is far from self-hatred and debasement. It really says that our self is worthy of being motivated by a noble purpose, and this sometimes requires us to willingly skip some otherwise acceptable activities.

## How Inferiority Masquerades as Pride

Closely connected with true and false denial is true and false humility. Some of us are afraid to have a good self-image for fear we will become proud and therefore sinful. And, in fact, the Bible tells us pride is sin. But pride should not be confused with a high sense of personal worth or self-esteem. Consider the following verse:

"I say to every man among you not to think more highly of himself than he ought to think, but to think so as to have sound judgment" (Romans 12:3 *NASB*). In other words, the Bible says pride is an inordinate self-esteem that either exaggerates our virtues or minimizes others in an attempt to place us on a higher level.

What usually is behind such pride? Once two of Jesus' disciples requested that in his future kingdom they should sit at his right and left hand (Mark 10:35-45). They seemed proud. They thought they were better than all the other apostles and deserved the very best positions. But, in reality, they were probably afraid they wouldn't get their just reward, so they had better nail it down ahead of time! If they hadn't been fearful and anxious of losing out, they would not have made such a request.

Behind this type of pride we find unconscious feelings of weakness and inadequacy. The pride is a way of trying to bolster our sagging self-image by feeling superior to others.

### How Inferiority Masquerades as Humility

Conversely, much so-called humility is also just a cover-up for feelings of worthlessness. The person who constantly apologizes for himself is often reflecting a self-condemning, self-pitying depression rather than a healthy form of biblical humility. These people often fall prey to teachings which, however well-meant, debase our worth. Consider the following from a widely read devotional book:

"Those who have been in tropical lands tell us that there is a big difference between a snake and a worm, when you attempt to strike at them. The snake rears itself up and hisses and tries to strike back—a true picture of self. But a worm offers no resistance; it allows you to do what you like with it, kick it or squash it under your heel—a picture of true brokenness. Jesus was willing to become just that for us—a worm and no man. And he did so, because that is what he saw us to be, worms having forfeited all rights by our sin, except to deserve hell. *And he now calls us to take our rightful place as worms for him and with him.* "[3] (Italics ours.)

Here we are exhorted to be "worms for Jesus." We're told we should be willing to be kicked and squashed and to forfeit all our rights. It is true, of course, that we are to take our proper places of submission before God. And it's also true that we are to respect others and avoid selfishness. Perhaps the writer means this, but his word choice suggests self-debasement is a virtue.

### True Humility

True humility is very different from this. It realistically recognizes our worth and abilities, without either over- or underestimating their importance. It recognizes that God is the originator of these gifts and that he entrusts them to us. We should be thankful and feel good that he has given us certain abilities, but we should also give God credit for distributing them to us in his love and wisdom. This keeps us from trying to rise egotistically above others.

## Self-Liberation

In contrast to self-hate and self-abasement, the Bible says we are to liberate our *renewed* selves. Our unique personalities, made in God's image, marred by the fall, and radically changed through Christ, need to grow and mature and find their full expression.

Paul says, "I can do all things in him who enables me" (Philippians 4:13, *RSV*).

Here he shows how the divine and human merge. Paul does not say, "Christ does everything; I do nothing." Nor does he say, "I do everything; Christ does nothing." He emphasizes that his renewed ego in union with Christ does what God wants him to do. He speaks of a divine-human relationship. In Philippians 2:13 he says, "It is God who works in you both to will and to do of his good pleasure." God works *in our egos* so that we can do what he wants. Again, it is a unifying relationship: he works in us, and as he works in us (our renewed egos) we do what he wants. God and our renewed egos work together.

Of course, if we try to live for God without his help, we will fail. But *with him* our renewed ego succeeds. This is why Jesus says if we "abide in him" and he "in us," we bear much fruit. But apart from Him, we can "do nothing" (John 15:5). The "nothing" here refers to works of spiritual value.

True and proper self-expression allows us to function according to our created uniqueness and our special giftedness.

### "I Am Unique"

*Could be a new intro on Temperaments*

David the psalmist wrote: "You made all the delicate, inner parts of my body, and knit them together in my mother's womb. Thank you for making me so wonderfully complex! It is amazing to think about. Your workmanship is marvelous—and how well I know it. You were there while I was being formed in utter seclusion! You saw me before I was born and scheduled each day of my life before I began

*His workmanship*

to breathe. Every day was recorded in your Book!" (Psalm 139:13-16, *TLB*).

Here David says God intricately planned every detail of our created existence. He laid out a genetic plan for the structure of our bodies and our personalities. And no two of us are exactly alike! God takes great pleasure in the uniqueness of his world. Just as he has combined vastly different physical properties of the universe to display his creative ability, our incredible individuality also reflects His divine design.

In the physical world, God beautifully merges light and dark, heat and cold, mountain and valley, and ocean and desert to provide a taste of his creative genius. The psalmist wrote:

"The heavens are telling the glory of God; they are a marvelous display of his craftsmanship. Day and night they keep on telling about God. Without a sound or word, silent in the skies, their message reaches out to all the world. The sun lives in the heavens where God placed it and moves out across the skies as radiant as a bridegroom going to his wedding, or as joyous as an athlete looking forward to a race! The sun crosses the heavens from end to end, and nothing can hide from its heat" (Psalm 19:1-6, *TLB*).

In the realm of human personality we see the same unique reflections of God's glory. In biblical times he used both an intellectual like Paul and an impulsive fisherman like Peter. In our day he continues to use widely different personalities. We see various aspects of his character and ministry reflected in the quiet and sensitive person; the aggressive, confident one; the scholarly, reflective type; the creative thinker; the faithful, plodding type; the "leader;" and the "average man."

### "I Am Gifted"

God purposely created us with different abilities and gifts. Quite clearly he isn't interested in building "Christian robots." He wants a band of committed followers who each add something distinctive to his creation.

Paul writes: "Just as there are many parts to our bodies, so it is with Christ's Body. We are all parts of it, and it takes every one of us to make it complete, for we each have different work to do. So we belong to each other, and each needs all the others. God has given each of us the ability to do certain things well. So if God has given you the ability to prophesy, then prophesy whenever you can—as often as your faith is strong enough to receive a message from God. If your gift is that of serving others, serve them well. If you are a teacher, do a good job of teaching. If you are a preacher, see to it that your sermons are strong and helpful. If God has given you money, be generous in helping others with it. If God has given you administrative ability and put you in charge of the work of others, take the responsibility seriously. Those who offer comfort to the sorrowing should do so with Christian cheer" (Romans 12:4-8, *TLB*).

In other words, we all have a place in the Body of Christ. Each of us is a "member" of the Body. Some of us are "arms," some are "eyes," some are "brains," some are "fingers," and some are "little toes." But each of us has a divinely given role. And the purpose of that role is not to reduce ourselves to nothing—it is to help each other grow!

### Practical Hints Toward Self-Liberation

"This all sounds good," you say, "but how can I make it work? On a practical level, how do I liberate my renewed self?" All growth, of course, takes time. But there are some principles that can help promote our growth. First, *our attitude must be self-love, not self-hatred.* And this attitude rests on far more than the optimistic admonitions of modern psychology! Instead, it's based on the great, broad biblical truths about our true nature. We can love ourselves because we are God's creation. We can love ourselves because God loves us. And we can love ourselves because he tells us to. The Bible makes it clear that we are to positively value both ourselves and one another. If God loves us and we degrade ourselves, we contradict his evaluation.

Second, we should not only love ourselves, *we should*

*expect something of ourselves.* Of course, we shouldn't expect Christian virtues before we have placed our faith in Christ. And we shouldn't expect dynamic Christian living without the power of the Holy Spirit and a knowledge of biblical teachings. But we should expect good performance when our renewed selves are enlightened and strengthened by the Holy Spirit. Though we often fail, we know we will continue to mature and grow; God himself will see to that. Paul says, "For I am confident of this very thing, that he who began a good work in you will perfect it until the day of Christ Jesus" (Philippians 1:6, *NASB*).

Finally, *we must repudiate our fallenness, without repudiating ourselves.* Galatians 5:24 says, "Those who belong to Christ Jesus have crucified [*i.e.,* repudiated] the flesh with its passions and desires" (*RSV*). We have seen that the self and the flesh are not the same. As we see our inhibiting anxieties and selfish cravings, we should put those things in God's perspective. We should honestly acknowledge their existence, but see that they contradict and hinder our true desire to become what our Father intends. At the same time, when we experience feelings of love, inner contentment, and proper self-discipline, we should accept and welcome these feelings as the natural product of our renewed selves through the influence of the Holy Spirit.

God has made us new. We shouldn't hide or be afraid of our new selves. And we shouldn't try to obliterate our selves. We should confidently yet humbly display our regenerated lives for the world to see. Jesus himself called us the "salt of the earth" and exhorted us to "let your light so shine before men that they may see your good works, and glorify your Father who is in heaven" (Matthew 5:16). God wants us to develop the potential he has built into us so that he can be glorified.

## Doing What Comes Naturally

At this point we add a word of caution: the process of Christian growth is a life-long process. At the same time the Holy Spirit is enlightening our renewed selves, we still have a battle with our old ways. Christian growth doesn't come just by "doing what comes naturally." Sometimes good comes easily but sometimes bad comes just as easily!

We tend to go to ridiculous extremes. While we sometimes frustrate ourselves by falling into the trap of self-depreciation, we can also lull ourselves into overconfidence and assume, "If it feels good, do it." The Bible warns clearly of this error. Jeremiah wrote, "The heart is deceitful above all things, and desperately wicked; who can know it?" (17:9) We must beware of such self-deception!

It is easy to become complacent or to rationalize our sins and self-centeredness away. We must be continually sensitive to this ever-present tendency. To avoid it, we must measure our deeds by biblical standards and heed the corrections and exhortations of our Christian friends and teachers. In this way we can be sure our growth is positive and can avoid unknowingly slipping into harmful patterns of thought or action.

FOOTNOTES

1. Some Bible scholars consider the "old man" the same as the "flesh," but this doesn't seem consistent with its biblical usage. Romans 6:6 says the old man was crucified at conversion. Colossians 3:9 says we have already "laid aside" the old man (English past tense), implying it has already happened at conversion, as in the other passages.

2. Solomon, Charles, *Handbook of Happiness* (Denver: Grace Fellowship Press, 1971) p. 93.

3. Hession, Roy, *The Calvary Road* (London, England: Christian Literature Crusade, 1950) p. 15.

# 7

# The I O U Complex

Many people unconsciously keep a kind of mental accounting ledger. On one side they list their faults and failures, on the other they put down offsetting successes and forgivenesses. When the positive outweighs the negative they are happy. When the bad outweighs the good, they begin to experience a "psychological I O U." They think, "I'm bad, and I'll have to pay for that by getting some kind of punishment."

All of us experience a little of this feeling. When a financial reversal, accident, or illness strikes, don't we sometimes wonder what we've done to bring it on? The implication is, of course, that we are being punished for our misbehavior. This is another part of the guilt emotion.

Jesus' disciples once saw a blind beggar and asked, "Who sinned, this man or his parents that he should be born blind?" (John 9:2, *NASB*). They could only understand his grievous handicap as a kind of payoff for someone's sins. Jesus refuted this notion and said, "Neither, but he was born blind in order that the workings of God should be manifested—displayed and illustrated—in him" (John 9:36, *Amp.*).

As we have seen, most of our fears of punishment are learned in early childhood. Later they are transferred from our parents to all authority figures, including God.

## Does God Punish Wrongdoing?

Since this is such a universal phenomenon, we immediately wonder: Is such fear justified? As we turn to the Bible, we find it is for some people. Jesus, the ultimate authority on the subject, teaches that God *does* punish sin and wrongdoing. He spoke of those who go into eternal punishment as well as those who go into eternal life (Matthew 25:46). He said hell is a place of "weeping and gnashing of teeth," "where the worm never dies, and the fire never goes out" (Matthew 24:51; Mark 9:48, *TLB*).

### A Remnant of the Primitive Past?

Some think the fear of punishment and hell is a remnant from man's primitive past and therefore has nothing to do with modern man. They don't believe God is active in society in any personal sense. In God's place they put man-made moral regulations, and, of course, God couldn't punish us for breaking man-made standards. It can't be *that bad* a crime.

But the Bible runs directly counter to this view. It reveals God as a personal being who set in motion the entire universe as well as establishing our moral principles. He knows the human havoc caused by violation of these standards, and as any righteous judge must dispense appropriate punishment for lawlessness and sin.

### The Divine Dilemma

This poses a problem for God: on the one hand, he is completely righteous and holy; on the other, he is totally loving. These attributes seem to clash at times. How can a loving God doom humans to eternal punishment? But at the same time how can a righteous God avoid punishing law-breakers?

Jesus Christ and the gospel is the answer. God sent his Son Jesus to live a perfect life and then to die for our wrongs. "He personally carried the load of our sins in his own body when he died on the cross, so that we can be finished with sin and live a good life from now on. For his wounds have healed ours!" (1 Peter 2:24, *TLB*).

Even the Old Testament foresaw this divine solution. Centuries before Jesus, the Prophet Isaiah wrote, "All of us like sheep have gone astray. Each of us has turned to his own way; but the Lord has caused the iniquity of us all to fall on him" (Isaiah 53:6, *NASB*). In other words, Jesus died in our place. In doing this, he freed us from the punishment we deserve and allowed God's love to continue to reach out to us.

## Was This the Final Payment?

Even though Jesus and the apostles committed this message to the Christian church, many sections of the church have been slow to accept its full implications. They have implied that Jesus' death for us was not sufficient to take away all punishment—there are still some things we must do. Yet the Bible makes nothing clearer than the finality and totality of Jesus' atonement.

The *Letter to the Hebrews* contrasts Christ's sacrifice of his life with the continual animal sacrifices offered by Jewish priests. Jesus, we read, "does not need daily, like those high priests, to offer up sacrifices, first for his own sins, and then for the sins of the people, because this he did *once for all* when he offered up himself" (Hebrews 7:27, *NASB*). Paul adds: "For the death that he died, he died to sin, *once for all*" (Romans 6:10, *NASB*). This suffering and death was a final event that never needs to be repeated.

The reason it never needs to be repeated is that it left no sin unpaid. The Apostle John says, "He himself is the propitiation (i.e., satisfactory sacrifice) for our sins, and not for ours only, but also for those of the *whole world*" (1 John 2:2, *NASB*). On this basis, Paul wrote that God has "forgiven us *all* our transgressions" and John could chime in: "The blood of Jesus cleanses us from *all* sin" (Colossians 2:13, *NASB*; 1 John 1:7, *NASB*). The writer to the Hebrews repeats God's promise given to Jeremiah: "I will *never again* remember their sins and lawless deeds" (Hebrews 10:17, *TLB*).

### The Bill-Consolidation Loan

Some loan companies advertise "bill-consolidation loans." They give you one lump sum to pay off all your smaller bills. Christ's atonement for our sins works in a similar way. With one gigantic sum (his death on the cross) he cancels all our outstanding moral bills. But there is one tremendous difference—his payment is a *gift* we never need to repay.

There's only one condition for settling our sin-account: we must admit our sin-liability and ask the help of the only One who can pay our obligations. It's a gift, but we must be willing to receive it.

### You Can't Spank a Child Just Once

It's one thing to know that Jesus has paid the penalty for our sins, and it's quite another to feel totally free from punishment. As children, most of us were punished for misdeeds. Our parents weren't able to say, "We are going to punish you one time, and it will take care of all your past, present, and future disobedience." Even if they could have done this, we wouldn't have wanted all that punishment at one time! As a result, we were punished each time we misbehaved. When we became adults we continued to expect punishment. If misdeeds accumulate and no punishment comes, our suspicion grows. We become afraid that when punishment finally arrives, we're *really* going to get it. This causes us to be afraid of God.

### Discipline or Punishment?

We need to realize that once we believe in Christ, God will never punish us for wrongs. He punished Christ in our place. God does *correct* or *discipline* us. This is entirely different. Punishment is payment for misdeeds, and Christ made that payment 2,000 years ago. Now God only corrects us as a loving Father.

When we do things that will harm ourselves, others, and God's work on earth, God corrects or disciplines us to rid us of these faults. Sometimes we receive correction from reading something in the Bible. Sometimes God uses others to helpfully instruct us. And sometimes he uses circumstances to show us things that need to change.

This discipline is quite different from punishment. Because God's anger toward our sin was all vented on Christ at the cross, God now acts toward us completely in love. A comparison of the following biblical passages illustrates the great difference between God's punishment and his discipline. God *never punishes* the Christian, but he *does discipline.*

*To the Christian (discipline):* "My son, do not reject the discipline of the Lord, or loathe his reproof; For whom the Lord loves he reproves, even as a father the son in whom he delights" (Proverbs 3:11, 12, *NASB*).

*To the Non-Christian (punishment):* "Behold, the day of the Lord is coming, cruel, with fury and burning anger, to make the land a desolation; and he will exterminate its sinners from it. Thus I will punish the world for its evil, and the wicked for their iniquity; I will also put an end to the arrogance of the proud, and abase the haughtiness of the ruthless" (Isaiah 13:9, 11, *NASB*).

*To the Christian (discipline):* "Those whom I love, I reprove and discipline; be zealous therefore, and repent" (Revelation 3:19, *NASB*).

*To the Non-Christian (punishment):* "And these will go away into eternal punishment, but the righteous into eternal life" (Matthew 25:46, *NASB*).

*To the Christian (discipline):* "Bear what you have to bear as 'chastening'—as God's dealing with you as sons. No true son ever grows up uncorrected by his father. For our fathers used to correct us according to their own ideas during the brief days of childhood. But God corrects us all our days for our own benefit, to teach us his holiness" (Hebrews 12:6, 7, 10, *Ph.*).

*To the Non-Christian (punishment):* "The Lord knows how to rescue the godly from temptation, and to keep the unrighteous under punishment for the day of judgment" (2 Peter 2:9, *NASB*).

Notice the differences. Discipline is not a means of justice. It's God's way of maturing us. Discipline focuses on the future and is done in love, while punishment focuses on the past and reflects God's anger. The accompanying table summarizes these distinctions.

Unfortunately, none of us grew up with parents who disciplined us perfectly. Sometimes our parents punished in anger and frustration or motivated us by guilt. Other times they threatened or subtly rejected us. For that reason, we sometimes have trouble seeing the difference between God's punishment and his discipline.

I counseled one woman who had some very negative childhood experiences. Her father drank heavily and had other serious problems. Her poor relationship with her father carried over into her relationship with God. She feared him just like she did her father. She told me how she tried to pray daily, but her prayers didn't seem to go beyond the roof. Nothing seemed to help. God seemed a million miles away.

Sensing her unhealthy fear of God, I said, "Why don't you forget praying for a while?" Immediately she exclaimed, "If I didn't pray every day, I would be afraid God would strike me dead!" Then she broke into tears.

Such fear! Her image of God was that of a harsh, punitive father. After talking through her feelings toward her father, she slowly started to understand God's love. She began to realize her sins had been paid for by Christ, and that her motives for reading the Bible and praying shouldn't be to placate a vengeful God. Instead, she should want to experience his great love.

One morning she entered my office with a radiant smile and said happily, "I prayed and enjoyed it for the first time

|  | PUNISHMENT | DISCIPLINE |
|---|---|---|
| *Purpose* | To inflict penalty for an offense, to pay back for wrongs | To correct and promote positive growth |
| *Focus* | Past misdeeds | Future correct deeds |
| *Attitude* | Righteous anger | Love |
| *Resulting emotion in the punished or disciplined person* | Fear, guilt, and hostility | Security |

in my life this morning!" "Why?" I asked. "Because I wanted to get to know my heavenly Father!" she replied.

This woman was finding that our heavenly Father doesn't punish his children as her own father had. God loves us, and when that love requires discipline he does it lovingly. Because of this, we need never fear punishment. John summarizes this principle perfectly:

"We need have no fear of someone who loves us perfectly; his perfect love for us eliminates all dread of what he might do to us. If we are afraid, it is for fear of what he might do to us, and shows that we are not fully convinced that he really loves us" (1 John 4:18, *TLB*).

We should *never* be afraid of God. Christ has done everything necessary to totally reconcile us to God.

### Respect and Fearful Anxiety

Sometimes we are afraid of God because we confuse the meanings of *respect* and *fear*. The Bible sometimes uses the word "fear" to describe a form of *fearful anxiety*. At other times it uses "fear" positively to mean *respect*. In the following passages "fear" means "respect."

"The fear of the Lord is the beginning of wisdom, and the knowledge of the Holy One is understanding" (Proverbs 9:10, *NASB*).

"The fear of the Lord leads to life, so that one may sleep satisfied, untouched by evil" (Proverbs 19:23, *NASB*).

But here "fear" means *fearful anxiety:*

"It is a fearful thing to fall into the hands of the living God" (Hebrews 10:31).

"For you have not received a spirit of slavery leading to fear again, but you have received a spirit of adoption as sons by which we cry out, 'Abba! Father!' " (Romans 8:15, *NASB*).

"For God has not given us a spirit of timidity, but of power and love and discipline" (2 Timothy 1:7, *NASB*).

When John says "we need have no fear," he means we should never have any *fearful anxiety* in our relationship to God. The reason is that Christ has already paid for our misdeeds and we are fully accepted by God. Since no English translation consistently differentiates between fearful anxiety and respect, we need to understand the context of each use to know which meaning is intended. God does not want us to be afraid of him; he does want us to respect him.

### Rewards

Some Christians struggle needlessly over the matter of biblical rewards. They equate heavenly rewards with earning God's favor and loss of rewards with punishment. While the Bible clearly teaches we may receive rewards in the future life, it does not equate the lack of these rewards with punishment. As Paul explains one type of reward:

"For no man can lay a foundation other than the one which is laid, which is Jesus Christ. Now if any man builds upon the foundation with gold, silver, precious stones, wood, hay, straw, each man's work will become evident; for the day will show it, because it is to be revealed with fire; and the fire itself will test the quality of each man's work. If any man's work which he has built upon it remains, he shall receive a reward. If any man's work is burned up, he shall suffer loss; but he himself shall be saved, yet so as through fire" (1 Corinthians 3:11-15, *NASB*).   Since Christ paid for all sins, he paid for the sin of not fulfilling our potential and not serving him as effectively as we could. Romans 8:1 states clearly: "There is therefore now *no condemnation* for those who are in Christ Jesus" (*NASB*). Therefore, no judicial punishment for sin can come to the Christian. However, those who fail to fulfill their potential do suffer a loss of reward in the future life.

### *Not a Contest*

Sometimes we have trouble grasping this because we subconsciously imagine a heavenly scene similar to the crowning of a beauty queen. When the judges announce the winner, she screams in delight and her competitors hug and kiss her and seem just as joyful. Yet we know that inside they are disappointed and crestfallen; their smiles often hide inner tears and pain. Similarly, we think we may watch God give a giant reward to some friend while we feel left out or put down. But this is a faulty conception that causes much undue anxiety.

Because God knows our weakness in this area, the Bible does not stress future rewards. God doesn't want us to try to *earn* rewards like we would wages, grades, or honors. When he does grant us our rewards, we will be in a state of incredible perfection and our motives and reactions will produce wholehearted consent. We won't feel one twinge of competition or comparison.

Fear of punishment *can* motivate us to arduous activity. And it often does. But activity and accomplishments are not the real answer. Unless our motives are free from fear, our lives lack inner fulfillment no matter how outwardly success-ful we appear.

# 8

# The Silent Treatment

Undoubtedly, you've awakened on mornings feeling bright and optimistic. You have read your Bible, enjoyed a good time with your family, spent a good day on the job (away or at home), and thought "It's great to be a Christian." You felt close to God and assumed he felt the same toward you. You felt approved, worthy, and accepted. In short, you felt "in fellowship" with him.

Other days are entirely different. When morning rolls around you wish the sun hadn't come up. Feeling grouchy, you roll over and try to catch a few more winks of sleep. When you finally make it up, you gripe at your mate, fuss at the kids, and almost wreck your car on the way to work. On the job everything goes badly. You lose your temper or ignore an opportunity to share your faith. To make matters worse, you commit some specific wrong in thought or action. That night you feel discouraged, angry, depressed. God seems far away. You feel unworthy, unloved and deserving of punishment. You expect God to frown down upon you. You feel "out of fellowship" with him.

These feelings of distance or rejection are another part of the guilt emotion. Even after we realize God wants us to have a positive self-image and to be free from fear of punishment, many of us are still afraid of alienating him or losing his approval.

76

Like all guilt feelings, the fear of displeasing God and losing his approval is learned in early life. As children, we came to expect temporary rejection when our attitudes or actions weren't acceptable. To correct us, our parents probably began with reason and instruction. When this failed, they threatened us with punishment or tried to shame and pressure us into altering our behavior. When this happened, we clearly sensed their displeasure and knew they were upset. Suddenly there were barriers between us. We experienced a kind of "silent treatment" and felt "out of fellowship" with them.

Coming into adulthood, we bring these feelings with us. When we fall short of God's standards, we expect him to be angry and cold. We think he will subtly withdraw his love or threaten us with punishment. While we may not fear he will punish us with tragedy, we may unconsciously expect a retaliation of silence and withdrawal. We can't believe God will be as "close" to us when we are bad as when we're good. Since rebellion against our parents caused them to react with anger and blocked communication, we assume the same is true with God.

This carryover from our human parents to God was shown at a meeting I led. When I spoke about our transference of attitudes from our parents to God, a woman raised her hand and said, "Sometimes when I pray I imagine God behind a newspaper. That's where my father spent his time and I imagine God must do the same!"

### The Ninety Percent Hero and Five Percent Flop

Happily, this painful feeling is totally unfounded. God does not reject us or withdraw from us because we do wrong. The feeling that he does stems from our false assumption that God accepts us on the basis of our daily goodness. It implies that sometimes we are sufficiently good to merit God's approval while on other days we are not.

This thinking is fabricated on a "percentile brand" of Christianity. We realize, of course, that we fall short of God's perfection in varying degrees. Some people are relatively better than others, and on some days we perform better than others. Because of this we tend to rank ourselves and others on a "spiritual scale." We might, for instance, rank some great Christian hero at ninety percent and a notorious failure at five percent. On a good day we might rate ourselves at seventy percent and on a bad day at ten. But the crucial question is: Does God accept the "ninety percent" Christian hero more genuinely than the "five percent" flop when both are true Christians? Do ups and downs of daily goodness make us more or less approved by God? To answer this we turn again to the Bible.

### How Good Is Good?

In Galatians Paul writes, "Cursed be everyone who does not abide by all things written in the book of the Law, to perform them" (Galatians 3:10, *NASB*). James tells us: "And the person who keeps every law of God, but makes one little slip, is just as guilty as the person who has broken every law there is" (2:10, *TLB*). Here we see we must do "*all* things written in the book of the Law" in order to merit God's acceptance.

### How Bad Is Bad?

The Bible doesn't distinguish between "little" and "large" sins; it views them all alike. Unconscious attitudes are just as offensive to God as outward vile reactions. In fact, the Bible lists sins we think of as "minor" and insufficient to alienate us from God right alongside those we think are terrible. Look at the list of sins Paul mentions in his Galatian letter.

"But when you follow your own wrong inclinations your lives will produce these evil results: impure thoughts, eagerness for lustful pleasure, idolatry, spiritism (that is, encouraging the activity of demons), hatred and fighting, jealousy and anger, constant effort to get the best for yourself, complaints and criticisms, the feeling that everyone else is wrong except those in your own little group—and there will be wrong doctrine, envy, murder, drunkenness, wild parties, and all that sort of thing. Let me tell you again as I have before, that anyone living that sort of life will not inherit the kingdom of God" (Galatians 5:19-21, *TLB*).

What a variety of human behaviors Paul lumps together and equally condemns! Occult involvement (frequently accompanied in the ancient world by drug addiction) is listed next to a bitter attitude. And drunkenness is listed beside envy. Similar lists appear in Romans and Proverbs, where "the gossip" is mentioned next to "the hater of God," and the "lying tongue" is next to those "whose hands shed innocent blood" (Romans 1:29, 30; Proverbs 6:16, 17, *NASB*).

### It's What's Inside That Counts

If this wasn't enough, Christ also taught that our inner attitudes are as important as our outer actions! To hate is the equivalent of murder in God's sight, and to lust is the same as committing adultery! In the Sermon on the Mount Jesus said:

"Under the laws of Moses the rule was, 'If you kill, you must die.' But I have added to that rule, and tell you that if you are only angry, even in your own home, you are in danger of judgment! If you call your friend an idiot, you are in danger of being brought before the court. And if you curse him, you are in danger of the fires of hell" (Matthew 5:21-23, *TLB*).

In Luke 6:45 Christ said, "A good man out of the good treasure of his heart brings forth what is good; and the evil man out of the evil treasure brings forth what is evil; for his mouth speaks from that which fills his heart" (*NASB*). The Bible clearly teaches that meeting God's requirements includes conformity of both outward acts and inner attitudes.

### Even What's Underneath Counts

We may think only "conscious" faults are serious enough to attract God's attention or offend his holy nature. If sin is on the unconscious level, we suppose it's not so bad and can't separate us from him. Yet there is no hint in the Bible that wrongs must be "conscious" to be sin. This misunderstanding arises from a confusion of our human perspective and God's divine viewpoint. We know, of course, that some human failures have especially bad effects on people. We know that some people are more openly rebellious. And we know that sometimes we are "better" than at others. But God doesn't fellowship with us on the basis of our good intentions, honest efforts, or "spirituality." He accepts us only on the basis of his character that demands one hundred percent perfection. Even an unconscious fault, while not seeming bad from our perspective, offends God and is sufficient to alienate us from him. The vital issue in terms of our relationship with God is *not* how hard we try, how *good* we are, or how *close* we come, but whether we have the one hundred percent righteousness God demands. If we do, we are acceptable to him; if we do not, we are *never* acceptable no matter how hard we try or how good and moral we may be.

John illustrates this when he says, "If we walk in the light as he himself is in the light, we have fellowship with one another, and the blood of Jesus his Son cleanses us from all sin" (1 John 1:7, *NASB*). John is saying that even when we are walking in the light—living as he wants us to—we *still* need cleansing from sin. We need to be pardoned for those repressed bad attitudes and those long-forgotten thoughts and deeds. Our lives are never for a moment totally free from sin. We always have some unconscious bad attitude or some hidden fault.

### What About the Positives?

We've seen that God's law encompasses all kinds of wrongs, both outward and inward. But God's law is more than a set of prohibitions; it also includes positive commands. In various places the Bible tells us: "Walk in love as Christ has loved us," "Be anxious for nothing," "Rejoice always," "Forgive each other just as God in Christ has forgiven you," and "Always give thanks" (Ephesians 5:2;

Philippians 4:6; 1 Thessalonians 5:16; Ephesians 4:32; 1 Thessalonians 5:18). Even if we could avoid all negative sins, we would still have to be totally loving, completely forgiving, always thankful, and never worrying if we were to live up to God's standards and merit his daily approval.

Obviously, these standards are impossibly high. By seeing just how high they are, it should be clear that no one can keep them all. Therefore, the most mature Christian in the world with no conscious failings is not one bit more acceptable to God at any moment than we are at our worst moments or than the most rebellious Christian.

There never has been any man—except Jesus Christ—who kept the law of God in its totality for even one day. If our daily acceptance by God were based on reaching these standards, every Christian should feel continually rejected.

## One Way of Acceptance

Unfortunately, many Christians think our daily acceptance by God comes on a different basis than our eternal acceptance. While they believe God forgave all the sins committed before they believed in Jesus Christ, they think they must earn daily acceptance to maintain their relationship. Consequently they feel quite secure about attaining eternal life but are filled with fear of God's displeasure on their daily conduct.

To help remove these fears, the Bible assures us that Christians are "*in Christ.*" It says, "There is therefore now no condemnation to those who are *in Christ Jesus*" (Romans 8:1, *NASB*). Suppose you put a piece of paper between the pages of a book, then close the book. Whatever happens to the book happens to the paper. If you throw the book away, you throw the paper away. If you put the book in a safe place, you safeguard the paper. If the paper is dirty and spotted, you don't see the dirt at all—you only see the book. The same is true of our position in Christ. When God looks on us, He sees us "in Christ." He doesn't see our dirt. He sees us as just as clean and pure as Jesus Christ himself. At one point Paul explained it this way:

"And that I may [actually] be found and known as in him, not having any (self-achieved) righteousness ... but possessing that [genuine righteousness] which comes through faith in Christ, the Anointed One, the [truly] right standing with God, which comes from God by (saving) faith" (Philippians 3:9, *Amp.*). If we are "in Christ" God cannot reject, condemn, or throw us out without throwing Christ out. As he accepts Christ, he accepts us.

In sharp contrast to the "Now he hears me, now he doesn't" type of acceptance, God's acceptance is unconditional. Because we are in Christ, God cannot even momentarily reject us, because he cannot reject his perfect Son. God laid our faults on him, punished him in our place, then credited his goodness to us. We are made acceptable by Christ's righteousness. Although our daily goodness varies, this basis of our acceptance *never* changes. That's part of the incredibly good news of the New Testament!

### What Happens When We Sin?

All this raises the question: "What actually happens to our relationship with God when we consciously sin?" At that moment we generally experience feelings of guilt. We either expect God to punish us, we feel he has in some way temporarily turned his back on us, or we feel a loss of self-esteem. We might imagine God saying something like, "I still love you, but since you have sinned, I am temporarily alienated from you."

God does not, of course, approve of what we have done, but is he *really* alienated from us? Actually, the feeling of alienation does not come from God. It is our human response to our rebellion. God accepts the Christian completely no matter what his current state of sin. We, however, imagine we are temporarily rejected and feel alienated from him. The feeling of alienation is actually just the product of our imagination. It is self-imposed.

Since we think God is like our parents, we expect him to temporarily reject us or "break fellowship" when we rebel. Then, when we repent, we imagine that we are once more totally accepted. But these feelings are simply our own mental gymnastics. God is accepting us the whole time. Look at the following charts.

Before salvation, sin erects barriers between ourselves and God. Because of his just and holy nature, God pronounces us worthy of punishment, alienation, and lowered self-esteem. This divine assessment of our human condition constitutes one-half of the barrier between God and man. Based on our sense of right and wrong and our childhood experiences with punishment and guilt feelings, we, too, erect barriers between us and God. These barriers are in the form of our expectations of punishment, rejection, and

### SIN BARRIERS BEFORE SALVATION

| | Barriers on God's side | Barriers on man's side | |
|---|---|---|---|
| GOD | 1. God's justice demands punishment of the guilty | 1. Man's knowledge of his guilt brings fear of punishment | MAN |
| | 2. God's holiness demands rejection of the unholy | 2. Man's knowledge of his lack of holiness brings a fear of rejection | |
| | 3. God's perfection demands devaluation of the imperfect | 3. Man's knowledge of his imperfection brings a loss of self-esteem | |

lowered self-esteem. In the diagram, God and man are headed in different directions.

When we become Christians, the barriers on God's side are totally removed. Christ's death did away with all of God's demands on forgiven man and he moved unhindered toward the new man. But now let's look at the other side of the barrier. Christ's death did not instantaneously remove our deeply ingrained fears of punishment, rejection, and lowered self-esteem. Many years of expecting punishment when we rebel doesn't immediately drop away. This leaves a barrier on our side. We want to hide from God because we fear his retaliation or rejection. When we rebel and hide, we naturally believe God is angry with us. But he isn't. There is no barrier on God's side. The only barrier is the one we imagine because of our childhood training. Even though we are turned away from God he is still moving toward us.

As we realize God's total acceptance of us, we can overcome the fear of God withdrawing fellowship and realize he never rejects us—not even for a moment. We can live in the

## SIN BARRIERS AFTER SALVATION WHEN WE FORGET THAT GOD TOTALLY ACCEPTS US

| | *Barriers on God's side* | *Barriers on man's side* | |
|---|---|---|---|
| GOD | Totally removed by Christ's death | Expectancy of punishment, rejection, and loss of self-esteem, all resulting from our early experiences with punishment | MAN |

move toward God. We react to his love and acceptance with a grateful, love-motivated response.

freeing awareness that there are now no barriers between God and man! When we recognize this we again want to

## SIN BARRIERS AFTER SALVATION WHEN WE HAVE FULLY APPLIED THE RESULTS OF CHRIST'S ATONEMENT

| *Barriers on God's side* | *Barriers on man's side* |
|---|---|
| Totally removed by Christ's death | Totally removed by the knowledge of God's total acceptance and for-giveness and by realizing God doesn't motivate by threats of punishment, rejection, and lowered self-esteem |

GOD                                                    MAN

### Does Goodness Ever Matter?

This understanding of God's great acceptance raises another question: since we are totally accepted, does it make any difference whether we are good or bad? It makes no difference as far as our divine acceptance, but it does make a world of difference in terms of our daily happiness and personal effectiveness. We will take a look at this in the next chapter.

# 9

# "If I Believed All That..."

After I presented the fact of God's full acceptance of Christians to a public gathering, a college student raised his hand and said, "If I believed all that, I'd really sin it up!" Many of us have the same reaction: We think, "If God doesn't hold my sins against me—why should I worry about them!"

## Those Wild Oats

Paul anticipated this when he wrote, "What shall we say then? Are we to continue in sin that grace might increase? May it never be! How shall we who died to sin still live in it?" (Romans 6:1, 2, *NASB*). Paul is saying that even though Christians are free from the divine penalty for sin, this doesn't justify a rebellious life. God's unconditional daily acceptance and his refusal to use the guilt and power-oriented corrective techniques of our parents doesn't mean we should "sin it up."

### *It Always Hurts*

In recent months our local newspaper reported the following events:

A forty-four-year-old intoxicated driver went the wrong direction up a freeway off-ramp and killed three people.
A college student fell to his death out of a fifth-story window while on an LSD trip.
An infant was born addicted to a dangerous drug because of her mother's own addiction.

Turning to the Bible, we find all sins have similar, built-in consequences. In Galatians Paul says, "Do not be deceived, God is not mocked; for whatever a man sows, this he will also reap. For the one who sows to his own flesh shall from the flesh reap corruption, but the one who sows to the Spirit shall from the Spirit reap eternal life" (Galatians 6:7, 8, *NASB*). First Peter 2:11 says, "Beloved, I urge you as aliens and strangers to abstain from fleshly lusts, which wage war against the soul" (*NASB*). The Old Testament declares that those who rebel against God "shall eat the fruit of their own way" (Proverbs 1:31, *NASB*).

Although we sometimes doubt it, every sin has some harmful effect on our physical or emotional lives. Some of the results are obvious. Excessive drinking, for example, results in lost jobs, broken homes, and tragic highway accidents. Drug addiction takes a similar toll. Other results of sin are more subtle.

Some people get drunk occasionally or smoke a little pot and observe no serious ill effects, yet both drinking and drugs can be deceptive. What starts as a "kick" can gradually become a life-style. And what started as an innocent "drunk" to let off tensions can quickly turn to tragedy.

### Hidden Sex Traps

Pre-marital sex relations can also cause much damage. I have counseled many young women who have had one or more sexual affairs. They wanted a deep and lasting relationship with a husband, but lacking confidence in their ability to secure this and being influenced by lax sexual mores, they settled for something less, thinking it would do no harm.

Some even thought they might be able to "graduate" their sexual partners into wedded mates.

Unfortunately, it doesn't work that way. The sexual relationship is the ultimate physical expression of total oneness. When the emotional commitment and unity of marriage is absent, the thrill of a sexual relationship soon deteriorates. Pressures and new attractions test the unity of the physical relationship, exposing its fragility. The temporary "security" and sexual thrills leave emotional wreckage and waste valuable years that could be spent building secure and meaningful relationships.

### Your Inner Enemies

Many people who are aware of the consequences of alcoholism, extra-marital sex relations, and drug abuse overlook the crippling effects of "minor" sins and negative attitudes. Psychosomatic illnesses like ulcers, headaches, and low-back pains are often triggered by resentments we have pushed into the unconscious where they supposedly would do no harm. Similarly, depression·and anxiety come in part from hidden anger.

Worry also causes problems. We worry about finances, education, children, ecology, the future, and a host of lesser things. Usually we try to convince ourselves worry isn't wrong; we may even name it "constructive planning." But the mental energy burned up by worry reveals its true nature. Worry tears at our personal wholeness and fulfillment. It robs us of joy in the present because of overconcern for the future. And it can dispatch us to bed physically and emotionally exhausted. For these reasons both Jesus and Paul instructed us not to be anxious: "Therefore do not be anxious for tomorrow; for tomorrow will care for itself. Each day has enough trouble of its own" (Matthew 6:34, *NASB*); "Be anxious for nothing, but in everything by prayer and supplication with thanksgiving let your requests be made known to God" (Philippians 4:6, *NASB*).

## Pride Comes Before A Fall

The proud and perfectionist individual provides graphic evidence of the effects of hidden sin. Driven by a need for acceptance and admiration, he becomes an excellent performer. His work is superior, or her home is immaculate. If he is the family breadwinner, he is "getting ahead in life." If she is a keeper of the home, her immaculate domain is her contribution to an orderly society. They are respected and admired, but perfectionist people generally have few, if any, close friends. They have such a need for acceptance they are afraid to relax and be themselves. They perform like computers and have comparable emotional warmth. They unwittingly isolate themselves from others because they have to invest so much time and energy building up and protecting their self-esteem. This keeps them continually under pressure and robs them of fulfilling relationships with others.

This often occurs in the Christian ministry. I have counseled ex-ministers, missionaries, and Christian workers who took pride in the superiority of their church or organization. They had extolled their alert congregations, sharp staff members, and vital Christianity while subtly demeaning the quality of other groups and churches.

Then, for one reason or another these people had to leave their ministries. All of a sudden they joined the ranks of the presumably less dedicated and less spiritual. The critical spirit and condemning attitude that used to be directed toward others was now turned on themselves, causing guilt, further failure, and loss of self-esteem. While they developed all sorts of rationalizations for leaving the Christian ministry, I sensed they hadn't really convinced themselves. They actually thought they were failures.

Thus the proud person loses either way. If he sets himself above others, he feels respected and important but he also feels isolated. Many dedicated and committed leaders in business and the church are lonely people. Trying to set an example for their followers, they are unable to relax and be themselves. This prevents close supportive relationships that are crucial to self-esteem and personal fulfillment. Although this condition is painful, it is more tolerable than the results of losing leadership. The perfectionist then turns his critical eye on himself and suffers from self-depreciation.

## No Man Is an Island

Sometimes we think what happens to us is strictly our own business, but sensitive people know this isn't true. We all communicate our hangups to other people and are in turn influenced by them. Parents, teachers, children, husbands, wives, and friends all strongly influence the lives of people around them.

### *Pass It On*

Perhaps the deepest imprints of human faults are made by parents upon their children. Moses told the Israelites that in some cases God visits the iniquity of "the fathers on the children, on the third and fourth generations" (Exodus 20:5, *NASB*). And he doesn't have to work to do it. When our sins and failures run their normal course, they harm future generations. Our hangups are passed to our children, who in turn pass them to their own. The New Testament says that parents' sins may cause specific problems like angry, resentful behavior or depression (Ephesians 6:4; Colossians 3:21).

A comparison of the offspring of two marriages clearly illustrates this. Over four hundred descendants of Jonathan Edwards, America's first great theologian, have been traced. Similarly, over twelve hundred offspring of a criminal named Jukes have been studied. Of the descendants of Jonathan Edwards: one hundred became ministers, missionaries, or theology teachers; one hundred became professors; over one hundred were lawyers and judges; sixty became doctors; and fourteen were college presidents.

Among the descendants of Jukes: one hundred and thirty were convicted criminals; three hundred and ten were professional paupers; four hundred were seriously injured or physically degenerated due to their life-styles; sixty were habitual thieves and pickpockets; seventeen were murderers; only twenty ever learned a trade, and half of these learned their trades in jail.*

What a potent illustration of biblical truth! While none of us is likely to generate such severe consequences, we can be sure our hangups will affect our children and our grandchildren.

The Bible also tells us the actions of children influence their parents. Some adolescents rebel and turn against their families. They think, "I can do what I want. It doesn't affect my family any more—I'm not home now." But their actions cause much heartbreak, especially for the mothers. Proverbs 10:1 confirms: "A foolish son is a grief to his mother" (*NASB*).

## Husbands and Wives

King Solomon was said to be one of the world's wisest men, yet in his later years he turned to idol worship. Who would guess this good king would succumb to this? But he did because of his pagan wives. Delilah did the same to Samson. His physical prowess was no match for her cleverness.

In similar but more subtle ways husbands and wives have incredible influence on each other. Both our obvious acts of sin and our immature personality characteristics damage our mates. The driven businessman who spends long hours at the office helps to drive his sensitive wife deeper into depression. The passive man who fails to take leadership in his home stirs anxiety, insecurity, and resentment in his wife. The domineering wife robs her husband of his masculinity, and the critical, angry wife adds to her husband's feelings of inadequacy. Proverbs says, "It is better to live in a corner of

---

* As in many historical studies, it's impossible to tell how much of the cause of problems in this family is due to genetic inheritance and how much is due to the family environment. It is obvious, however, that a good portion is due to the family influence.

an attic than with a crabby woman in a lovely home" (21:9, *TLB*).

### The Power of Words

Words have incredible power. They can stir up strife, defame character, ruin relationships, or change people permanently for the good.

James says: "So also the tongue is a small part of the body, and yet it boasts of great things. Behold, how great a forest is set aflame by such a small fire! And the tongue is a fire, the very world of iniquity; the tongue is set among our members as that which defiles the entire body, and sets on fire the course of our life" (3:5, 6, *NASB*). Later in the same chapter James writes, "And the seed whose fruit is righteousness is sown in peace by those who make peace" (verse 18).

Every human being possesses this powerful instrument. Our words can wound or heal. They can bring the "results of iniquity" or bear the "fruit of righteousness." This should lead us to watch our words—they are potent!

### Why Be Good?

Although sin doesn't alienate the Christian from God, it does have serious effects. Just as there are valid reasons for washing our hands before we eat, driving on the right side of the road and not playing with dynamite, there are good reasons for following biblical morality.

Combining the insights of the preceding chapters, we see that sins do not cause God to punish Christians, become angry with us, or reject us. And they do not make us worthless. But sins hurt us, our friends, our families, and the world around us. For the person who does not belong to Christ, his sins have the added consequence of separation from God. Sin is never worth its price. That's why God condemned it in the first place; he knew it wasn't for our good.

## EFFECTS OF SIN ON THE CHRISTIAN

| WHAT SIN DOESN'T DO | WHAT SIN DOES DO |
|---|---|
| 1. Bring punishment from God | 1. Brings loving correction and discipline from God |
| 2. Make God angry with us | 2. Interferes with our best personal adjustment, harms us, and eventually makes us unhappy |
| 3. Cause God to reject us, even temporarily | 3. Decreases our effectiveness in the world |
| 4. Make us worthless or valueless to God | 4. Damages the lives of others—especially those closest to us |
| 5. Cause God to make us feel guilty | 5. Brings loss of rewards in heaven |
| | 6. Brings conviction from God |

# 10

# Good Old Grace

Frustration was written across Carl's face. "I just can't get it all together," he said. "I read the Bible every day, I've helped several of my friends come to know Christ, and I don't have any gross faults. But something isn't right. No matter how hard I try, I'm never satisfied. I feel I haven't done enough and I just don't have the joy I used to feel."

A psychologist would quickly recognize Carl's tendencies toward perfectionism and his need for constant activity to feel worthwhile. He would probably give him some psychological label like "neurotic" and start helping him understand how childhood experiences programmed him for his frustrating life-style. The psychologist would probably be correct since an insatiable need to perform and a general lack of personal fulfillment both have their roots in early childhood.

But this is only the psychological side of Carl's problem. There is also a theological side. In adulthood these same attitudes are transferred onto God so that Carl always feels a little dissatisfaction in his Christian life. In fact, if the Apostle Paul had talked with Carl, he might have said, "Carl, you're feeling the same frustration so many feel today. You feel you have to do something to please God. But let me tell you something. No matter how hard you work or what you do, you'll never feel you've done enough! You're trying to relate to God by living under law. You don't understand the difference between 'law' and 'grace.' " Paul would be putting his finger on one of the central issues in the Christian life. Do we approach God on the basis of law and effort or by grace and love?

All we have said so far about freedom from guilt is built on a proper understanding of God's grace. Guilt's only lasting solution is found in the grace of God. To firmly cement in our minds, the foundations for guilt-free living, this chapter will look at the biblical teachings on law and grace. This is fundamental to overcoming guilt and building a positive self-image.

## Two Ways

According to the Bible, law and grace are opposite ways of approaching God. To make certain we understand the differences between the two, the New Testament devotes one entire book (Galatians) and half of another (Romans), plus many other passages, to this issue. We can summarize the differences by looking at their answers to these four questions: (1) How do we become acceptable to God? (2) How do we get daily blessings from God? (3) How does God motivate us? and (4) Where do we get the power to live as God wants us to?

### Celestial Brownie Points

The most basic difference between law and grace is how we get God's acceptance. *Law says: Perform so you will be accepted. Grace says: You are accepted, now you can perform.* The law lists numerous specific requirements we must meet to merit either eternal salvation or daily fellowship.* Under grace, we are accepted first because Christ died for us, then we naturally tend to perform as God wants. We per-

---

* This is not to imply that men were ever saved by law-keeping. During Old Testament times people were saved by faith in God on the basis of Christ's future atoning death.

form not to earn acceptance but because we are accepted. Paul says, "And be kind to one another, tender hearted, forgiving each other, just as God in Christ also has forgiven you" (Ephesians 4:32, *NASB*). Note the order of grace: first acceptance, then performance. *After* we are accepted and forgiven, then we are encouraged to forgive others.

### The Big If

The second difference between law and grace involves daily blessings or rewards. The nation of Israel had to work to earn rewards from God. Listen to the words of Moses.

"If you fully obey all of these commandments of the Lord your God, the laws I am declaring to you today, God will transform you into the greatest nation in the world. These are the blessings that will come upon you: blessings in the city, blessings in the field; many children, ample crops, large flocks and herds; blessings of fruit and bread; blessings when you come in, blessings when you go out" (Deuteronomy 28:1-6, *TLB*).

Notice the big "if." *If* Israel fully obeyed or performed they would get all these rewards. If they didn't, however, listen to what would happen:

"If you won't listen to the Lord your God and won't obey these laws I am giving you today, then all of these curses shall come upon you: curses in the city; curses in the fields; curses on your fruit and bread; the curse of barren wombs; curses upon your crops; curses upon the fertility of your cattle and flocks; curses when you come in; curses when you go out. For the Lord himself will send his personal curse upon you" (Deuteronomy 28:15-20a, *TLB*).

*Under law, we earn blessings. Under grace, God blesses us unconditionally, then we are encouraged to obey him.* Consider these two passages:

"How we praise God, the Father of our Lord Jesus Christ, who has blessed us with every blessing in heaven because we belong to Christ." "Since you have been chosen by God who has given you this new kind of life, and because of his deep love and concern for you, you should practice tenderhearted mercy and kindness to others. Don't worry about making a good impression on them but be ready to suffer quietly and patiently" (Ephesians 1:3; Colossians 3:12, *TLB*).

Here we see that spiritual rewards come because of Christ's work, not ours. Under law the formula is, "If you will do good, I will bless you." Under grace it's, "I have blessed you, now do good."

## Fear and Love

Just as law and grace have two different bases of acceptance and blessing, they operate under different motivations. *The law operates in large measure out of a fear motive.* Impending judgment was hanging over Israel if they disobeyed. If an individual disobeyed certain laws, he would face execution. If the nation disobeyed, it could be punished by a foreign army. Listen to how the people responded to God's initial giving of the law:

"For there was an awesome trumpet blast and a voice with a message so terrible that the people begged God to stop speaking. They staggered back under God's command that if even an animal touched the mountain it must die. Moses himself was so frightened at the sight that he shook with terrible fear" (Hebrews 12:19-21, *TLB*).

In great contrast, *grace removes fearful anxiety, and replaces it with a love motive.* The writer to the Hebrews makes this crystal clear.

"You have not had to stand face to face with terror, flaming fire, gloom, darkness, and a terrible storm. . . . But you have come right up into Mount Zion, to the city of the living God, the heavenly Jerusalem, and to the gathering of countless happy angels; and to the Church, composed of all those registered in heaven; and to God who is Judge of all; and to the spirits of the redeemed in heaven, already made perfect; and to Jesus himself, who has brought us his wonderful new agreement; and to the sprinkled blood which graciously forgives instead of crying out for vengeance as the blood of Abel did" (Hebrews 12:18a, 22-24, *TLB*).

John sums this up when he says: "We love, because he

first loved us" (1 John 4:19, *NASB*). God first extends his love to us, then we respond with loving obedience.

### Going It Alone

Our resources under law and grace are also different. *Under the law, the results are all up to us.* Moses said, "If *you* fully obey." *Under grace we have more than our own resources.* The Holy Spirit comes into our lives and helps our renewed ego function properly. This is the fourth distinction between law and grace. Paul says, "When the Holy Spirit controls our lives he will produce this kind of fruit in us: love, joy, peace, patience . . . self-control" (Galatians 5:22, 23, *TLB*).

### The Two Will Never Mix

One hot summer day I opened our refrigerator in search of a cold drink. Spotting what looked like fruit juice, I poured myself a glass. After one swallow I spit it out. I discovered that my young daughter had mixed some tomato juice with grape juice. The tomato juice was fine by itself, and the grape juice was all right too. But together they tasted horrible! Law and grace are much the same. Each has a distinct purpose, and serves that purpose well. The law frightens, condemns, and shows us we are moral failures. This prepares us for God's grace. Grace then steps in and rescues, heals, and forgives.

The New Testament tells us law and grace cannot mix any better than tomato and grape juice. It warns us that now that we are under grace, we should *never again* get entangled with the law. Peter told those who tried to mix law and grace: "Now therefore why do you put God to the test by placing upon the neck of the disciples a yoke which neither our fathers nor we have been able to bear?" (Acts 15:10, *NASB*). In his Galatian letter, Paul was just as firm: "It was for freedom that Christ set us free; therefore keep standing firm and do not be subject again to a yoke of slavery."

|  | LAW | GRACE |
|---|---|---|
| *Eternal acceptance* | Earned by our works | Given because of Christ's work |
| *Daily blessings* | Repeatedly earned by our works | Given because of Christ's work, and as a natural consequence of following biblical teachings |
| *Motivation* | Heavily based on fear | Based on love |
| *Source of power* | Our own efforts | The Holy Spirit enlightening and strengthening our renewed selves |
| *Result* | Condemnation | Salvation |

(Galatians 5:1, *NASB*). The reason law and grace can't mix is because their principles are antithetical.

It's impossible to *earn* acceptance and blessings if God has already given them to us. It's impossible to rely on the Holy Spirit if we are trying to go it alone. In addition to this, it's impossible to have salvation if we are under condemnation. We can summarize the conflicts of law and grace by looking at the accompanying chart.

### Lapsing Back Under Law

The New Testament and many theologians clearly teach we are under God's grace. This was the great affirmation of Martin Luther and other Reformation leaders. Yet human nature is such that Christians tend to slip back under subtle forms of law.

## When God Seems Far Away

Take the feeling of acceptance, for example. Don't we all have times when we feel especially close to God? On these occasions we usually feel an extra measure of acceptance, a kind of divine pat on the back. By contrast, when we have been rebellious or unresponsive we begin to feel God is starting to reject us. This is living "under law." When we aren't performing well we don't feel as much acceptance.

## All Those Rules

Because we have such a strong desire to feel accepted, we fool ourselves into thinking that specific performances will gain it. We often come up with extrabiblical standards of behavior. We forget we are acceptable through Christ and that we can't do one thing to earn more acceptance. Instead, we start looking around for highly visible ways of improving our standing before God. We begin to focus on specific lists of rules and start to judge ourselves and others by these lists.

Some churches, for example, habitually attack practices like drinking, smoking, and dancing. Others rule out movies or certain forms of dress. In past years, some churches forbade people of the opposite sex to swim together and considered makeup and seamless hose as "instruments of the devil." At least one religious sect still refuses to use the "horseless carriage" and other modern inventions.

Students who attend church colleges are sometimes required to promise to refrain from certain activities such as drinking and smoking. They are told that this is part of setting a Christian example to weaker Christians and the outside world, and that some of the activities, while not mentioned in the Bible, are clearly wrong.

At first this sounds sensible. Some activities are harmful. Many movies now present raw sex in living color, alcoholism takes a fierce toll, and smoking can be damaging to health. But setting prohibitions won't really resolve these issues. In fact, it can compound the problem. A heavy emphasis on external rules represents a lapse back under law. When we focus excessively on specific, visible, keepable rules of behavior, we begin to use them as a basis of determining how good we are. We want to *perform* to get acceptance. If we keep the rules we feel a bit more "righteous" or "spiritual." Those who fail to keep them are "sinful."

In this way, rules tend to create a rash of contradictions and hypocrisy. They cater to our craving for acceptance by our own efforts. They focus our attention on a few externals instead of the great biblical issues like love, justice, and humility. And they may lead to a form of pride and a tendency to judge others. In chapter fourteen we will present a biblical alternative to these impersonal codes.

### Wine That Makes the Heart Merry

Take drinking as an example. The Bible condemns drunkenness in such passages as Galatians 5:21, Ephesians 5:18, and Proverbs 23:20-21. But it does not command total abstinence. The Old Testament psalmist gave thanks to God for creating "wine which makes man's heart glad." And Jesus created a large quantity of wine when he performed his first public miracle at Cana. Some insist that he really created grape juice or some nonfermented beverage, but the Greek word used for wine is *oinos,* the same one Paul used when he said, "Do not get drunk with wine, but be filled with the Spirit" (Ephesians 5:18, *NASB*). To insist dogmatically that something Jesus created and drank in his day is now sinful for all Christians is contradictory.

Many choose to be total abstainers, with good reason, but to insist all Christians abstain is adding human tradition to biblical directives. We become guilty of requiring an external conformity not in the Bible. And in doing this we again turn the focus from what the Bible says is most important—our inner attitudes, our love, and self-control.

### *Those Cancer Sticks*

Smoking is another example. Medical evidence shows that smoking is linked to cancer and heart disease. Since the Bible says our body is the temple of the Holy Spirit, it seems best not to smoke. Yet why single out smoking as a special spiritual or moral issue to the exclusion of other equally harmful habits?

Overeating is just as bad. It endangers health, sets a bad example, and represents lack of discipline. But how many churches or schools have rules against being overweight? The great evangelist, D. L. Moody, weighed close to three hundred pounds. His friend, the famous English preacher Charles Spurgeon, smoked cigars at one period in his ministry. An anecdote has it that Moody once rebuked his cigar smoking friend about his bad habit, but for obvious reasons had little success! When we vigorously oppose one practice and are tolerant of another just as hurtful, we are trapped in a hypocritical mentality, not to mention the fact that we look ridiculous to the outside world.

### *Ashtrays in the Parish House*

Some churches have never had special rules concerning drinking, dancing, or smoking. In fact, they may serve beer at church picnics and have ash trays in their parish houses! But they may have very stringent rules concerning church membership, baptism, and communion.

A woman once complained to me that though she was unquestionably a Christian, she had to take two years of catechism classes before the church would allow her to participate in communion. Where do we find such a requirement in the Bible? This again is setting up an external human code to judge performance when no such code exists in the Bible.

### *Turning Off the Foreigner*

The results of this religious externalism have been disastrous in some foreign countries. As Western missionaries have carried Christianity to Africa and the Orient, they have often added rules from their own religious subculture. Coupled with elements of Western culture like architecture, clothing, and music, they presented the whole package as "Christianity." The result is that Christianity appears as an "American" or "Western" religion, and the church fails to send deep and strong roots into the local culture.

### Turning Off the Youth

Our own country recently witnessed a similar phenomenon. During the sixties a "youth culture" grew up, with long hair, rock music, new clothing styles, and rebellion against "the establishment." Some churches and groups, though not condoning drugs, immorality, or headstrong rebellion, sought to reach these youth without demanding a return to the musical tastes and clothing fashions of the 1950s. The result was an enthusiastic response. Former addicts and dropouts who turned to spreading the Christian message got national press coverage.

But other churches and groups seemed to think these youth were unacceptable to the church (and for all practical purposes, to God) unless they maintained a certain style of dress, clean-shaven faces, and the musical tastes of their parents. Sometimes they refused to allow them in their church unless they were "properly attired." These churches, of course, reached few, if any, segments of the secular youth culture. In fact, they lost many of their own to other Christian groups or to the drug world. In their religious externalism, these churches confused personal tastes and preferences with biblical morality and missed a golden opportunity to reach needy youth for Christ.

### "Harvey, If You Get Right With God, You'll Make Millions"

Another relapse to law comes when we try to perform well so God will reward us for our efforts. I once counseled an area manager for a well-known life insurance company— we'll call him Harvey. He had a lovely home, a fine family, and was active in his church. From all appearances he was successful. Unfortunately, his insurance region was doing poorly. He had difficulty recruiting qualified salesmen and his area was near the bottom in sales production.

He came to me discouraged, feeling his region's poor performance reflected a spiritual weakness in him. He thought God wasn't "blessing." Over a period of several weeks we got well acquainted and I began to help him understand his tendency to blame himself when things didn't go right.

I explained that God has a very different view of success than we do. While God obviously wants us to do our best in our vocational endeavors, he doesn't intend for all Christian businessmen to be the most successful in their fields. Then we discussed how we often confuse God's spiritual blessings with business success, financial prosperity, and physical health. The New Testament doesn't promise us health, prestige, or financial prosperity as a result of Christian living. We should do our best and be grateful for health, safety, and financial progress. But we shouldn't count these as direct rewards from God earned through good behavior. All of the Christian's direct rewards will come in heaven. While we're here on earth we will reap good and bad consequences for our actions, but these are not rewards or curses like Israel received under God's rule of law. They are the natural consequences of our actions.

Over the space of a few weeks Harvey's depression began to lift. He began to realize God wasn't punishing him for hidden faults by withholding sales. Then he went to a regional insurance meeting. One of the first men he met was a fellow Christian who said, "Harvey, I just straightened out my life with God last year, and you wouldn't believe how great sales have been since then. The Lord is really blessing." Immediately Harvey hit bottom again. All of our efforts to understand his spiritual life and professional work were derailed and we had to start over.

This experience is not uncommon. We usually choose the star athlete, the beauty queen, or the wealthy businessman as our "Christian heroes." The subtle implication (and sometimes not so subtle) is that if we were spiritually committed we, too, might become star athletes, beauty queens, or successful businessmen. When we don't, we are left feeling like second-class citizens who somehow just never had what it takes to earn God's highest blessings.

### Grace Is Pie In the Sky

Another lapse back under law comes when we see grace primarily as God's way to get us to heaven, but de-emphasize it as his way of dealing with us here and now. The reasoning goes like this: "Through Christ alone we are forgiven and accepted by God *for the future,* but for now we must do certain things to merit his favor, earn his blessings, and avoid his anger." The chart on page 106 summarizes this view.

By relegating much of God's grace to the future, we may think we are faithful to the teachings of the Bible. But we have made a fatal mixture of law and grace. What we fail to recognize is that God does not say we are under grace in the future—but that we are under it *now.* Paul writes, "You *are* not under law, but under grace" (Romans 6:14, *NASB*). Earning acceptance, fearful anxiety, and punishment are all a part of the law, not of grace. They cannot make us better *at any time.*

### Why Do We Do All This?

If God's grace is so great, why do we lapse back under law so easily? When God says he accepts us just as we are, why do we follow a way of life devised to earn his blessings or acceptance? When God says our only motive should be love, why do we choose to be afraid of him? And when God wants to strengthen us by the Holy Spirit, why do we want to go it alone? Why do we set up a spiritual life-style that reflects the principles of the law? And why do churches often add to the clear teachings of the Bible and ease Christians back under law? The next chapter takes a look at reasons for this pattern. There we will see why we unconsciously choose to live under the religious system known as legalism.

|  | FOR FUTURE LIFE | FOR HERE AND NOW |
|---|---|---|
| *How we are accepted* | Faith in Jesus Christ | Attending church, praying, reading the Bible, evangelizing, being good |
| *Our motive* | Love | Fear |
| *Our resource* | The Holy Spirit—he will keep us secure, so we can never be lost | Ourselves—we must love God, love others, be courageous, persistent, patient, gentle, Christlike |
| *What God does when we fail* | Graciously forgives us forever | Pays us back with financial reverses, illness, sometimes tragedy, and often "the silent treatment." |
| *What God does when we succeed* | Accepts us apart from this, but adds some rewards | Pays us back with answered prayers, money, good health, more love than we had before |

# 11

# Legalism Lies On The Couch

During the past few years I have presented the concepts of law and grace to a wide variety of audiences. In each group I find similar reactions. Some people agree wholeheartedly and say, "I've known those truths about God's grace and they have changed my life." Others say, "That's terrific! I've always thought I believed in grace but now I see how it really applies to my daily life. Already I feel a sense of relief and freedom." But a few always have a totally different reaction. They simply cannot bring themselves to accept these truths, much as they might enjoy the resulting release. They have been trained for years in an external, legalistic, rule-laden mentality which still clings to them. Large sections of the Christian church are still hemmed in by this and have limited their effectiveness as a result.

This shouldn't surprise us, for legalism has been a problem since the day Christianity was born. Even in Jesus' time there were highly legalistic religious leaders. In fact, some of the worst legalists and externalists who ever lived were operating then. They were known as Pharisees.

## World Champion Nit-Pickers

Jesus ran head-on into their legalism one Sabbath day when walking by a grainfield with his disciples. Being hungry, they stopped and picked some grain to eat. Although the law of Moses allowed this afternoon snack, the Pharisees became upset. They accused Jesus of four violations of the Sabbath-day rest. They said in picking the head of grain he was "harvesting." In rubbing it between his hands he was "threshing," and when he threw away the chaff he was "winnowing." And taken together the whole process was "preparation of food." This was one example of their fanatic attention to external details.

The Jewish Talmud had endless rules the Pharisees enforced in Jesus' day. Among these were the following Sabbath regulations:

You could carry food equivalent only to the weight of a dried fig, one goblet full of wine, one swallow of milk, water enough to moisten eye salve, or ink to write two letters.

You could not put out fire if your house was burning down, but you could carry out certain listed items.

If you threw a piece of fruit in the air, you could not catch it if Sabbath day overtook you at that moment—but you could catch it in your mouth and swallow it.

Needless to say, the Pharisees had converted a day of rest into a day of worry and strain. Jesus rejected their approach and said, "The Sabbath was made for man, not man for the Sabbath" (Mark 2:27, *NASB*). In other words, Jesus said God gave the Sabbath as a day of rest for man's benefit. It wasn't a day to test how many little rules we could keep to protect our religiosity and prove our spirituality!

Obviously, this sort of legalism is ridiculous. But I wonder if some of our rules won't look just as silly a few years from now. Some of the cherished rules of our great grandparents' generation certainly appear very laughable to us now! It seems that a Pharisaic, rule-laden mentality always manages to get some footholds in each new generation of the church, though it focuses on different issues. Men seem to have an incurable bent toward legalism; no matter how good God's grace sounds, some people want to sneak back under the law and take others with them. Why does this repeatedly happen?

The basic reason, of course, lies in our rebelliousness toward God. We don't like to be told we can do absolutely nothing to merit his approval so we design a life-style that gives us at least a little credit for our actions. We are too proud to admit our total inability to please God, so we con ourselves into thinking that we can do at least a few acceptable things.

But there's another reason for slipping back into legalism. This lies in our psychological makeup. We all have some inner needs for security and protection that seem to be met by slipping back to legalism. A look at some of those psychological dynamics can help us understand why we so readily choose legalism as a way of life even though it frustrates personal growth.

## That Hidden Childish Fear

Before birth we spent nine months in the safe, peaceful, controlled environment of our mother's womb. We had no pressures, no tensions, no dirty diapers and no feeding schedules. Suddenly, small and helpless, we were cast out into a big, threatening world. We had to face pain, illness, and frustration for the first time. And we didn't have all our needs immediately met. When we were wet and hungry, we couldn't help ourselves. When we wanted to grab an interesting object, we couldn't reach it. When we were sick we had to suffer through the pain. As we got older we were punished if we asserted our wills in violation of our parents'. And we had to follow their standards.

### *"My Parents Are Eighteen Feet Tall"*

Our parents were key forces in this process. By our standards they seemed huge and powerful. During the first few years of life they were five or ten times our size. Can you imagine having two eighteen-foot-tall giants assigned to you now as parents? This is exactly what every child must face! Parents could magically satisfy our hunger on an instant's notice or leave us crying in our cribs. They could help us reach things we wanted, but they could also become angry and punish us or deprive us of our wants. Even when we were teenagers they had power to buy our clothes, give us money, or lend the car—all on the condition that we play by their rules. Receiving these "blessings" was conditioned by our performance.

Several years of this arrangement instilled a deep and lasting lesson: "You are weak, the world is strong, there are powerful authorities in your life. If you want things to go well, you'd better please them." This left a deep core of fear of authority at the center of our lives.

If our parents combined sensitivity and love with firmness, we developed a relatively small amount of fear and much healthy respect for authority. But if they were easily upset and somehow punitive and rejecting, we developed a larger amount of fear. In either case, we developed a deeply ingrained core of fear that is triggered any time we come in conflict with authority. Our unconscious minds hold thoughts like, "You'd better watch out," "You can't trust them," or "They'll let you down."

### Conformists and Rebels

To placate this fear and keep it manageable, we developed different defenses and set up different life-styles. When we grew into adulthood we transferred these attitudes from our parents to the world in general and God in particular.

Some of us became obedient and conforming children in order to handle our fear. We reasoned, "If I do whatever my parents want, they won't reject me and will provide for my needs." As adults, we continue being obedient and conforming.

Some of us became efficient performers and achievers. We unconsciously reasoned, "If I always do a good job, better than my brothers and sisters, then my parents will be happy with me and love me." Some of us learned to take all the blame on ourselves. We thought, "If I blame my parents they will be angry with me. So I will play it safe. I will blame

myself no matter who did it. This way I will be loved."
Some of us tried to deny the fear entirely. We told ourselves:
"I'm not afraid of losing their love and I'll prove I'm not
afraid." We became strong-willed, rebellious, and super-
independent. We may have grown up following a daredevil
life-style, or engaged in a wild life of sin and rebellion to
prove we weren't afraid and weren't going to let any authority threaten us. But hidden under this external front of
confident assurance and defiance is the same childlike fear.

As adults, the reasons for developing these life-styles are
buried. But the childlike fear remains. This core of fear
explains one reason why we resist God's grace. Grace attacks
this fear head-on. It says, "You don't need to fear anymore.
Your parents may have failed you; I won't. Your parents
may have rejected you; I won't. You felt you had to earn
their love, but you don't have to earn mine." This sounds
great, and we really want it, but we have been programmed
for fear through many years of childhood. Each time we
start to operate on grace, countless fear-based experiences
stir in the recesses of our minds. The devil translates these to
say, "You'd better watch out; you can't trust God. Some
day he's going to get even with you."

It takes many new experiences and much growth to re-
place this inner fear with the mature love described by the
Apostle John. "There is no fear in love; but perfect love casts
out fear, because fear involves punishment, and the one who
fears is not perfected in love" (1 John 4:18, *NASB*).

### Pulling the Wool Over Your Own Eyes

This fear also explains why we want to operate under law:
we are programmed for it. By setting up a conforming type
of life-style or by stressing achievement, we hide our inner
failures. We repress our weaknesses in order to evade this
core of fear. We feel: "God must accept me because I keep
the rules, therefore I don't need to be afraid."

The problem, of course, is that any vile-hearted person
can conform to certain standards of dress, hair length, and
entertainment. And anyone who really tries can discipline

himself to attend church and pray once in a while. In contrast to this type of external conformity, *biblical directives* such as "be anxious for nothing," "love your enemy," and "walk in love as Christ has loved you" *require right inner motives.* Since we are afraid that God will reject us if he sees our real faults, we hide our inner failures and hope God will give us credit for our outward actions. It's natural that we do this since it has worked with people all our lives! Thus we make legalistic rules a way of pulling the wool over our own eyes and of hiding from our own faults.

Unfortunately, this repression causes more problems. Our hidden attitudes continue to stir up anxiety and depression and they can even lead to psychosomatic illnesses. Not until we recognize our total inability to merit God's approval and we are willing to be accepted only on the basis of Christ's imparted goodness can we be free from this need to deny our failings.

### False Security

Another stimulus to legalism is our need for security. While we all desire individuality and freedom of choice, we also want some guidelines and familiar structure. As children we learned to obey largely from *external* pressure. We were spanked, scolded, or denied some privileges. As we got older we received grades for good achievement or stars for Sunday school attendance. As teenagers we were warned of the dangers of following our own desires and taught to follow the directions and instructions of adults. For sixteen or eighteen years our actions were policed by the strengths of other people.

Some of this, of course, is necessary. Children do require external guidance, instruction, and correction. The problem comes when we expect God to take up where parents left off. We expect him to threaten, coerce, or punish us into conformity just like our parents. We think he tries to motivate us out of fear and guilt.

When we see God doesn't use external pressure—that we no longer have to obey to ward off punishment, rejection, or feelings of unworthiness—it scares us. Total freedom can be frightening. Although we enjoy the sense of liberty, we're afraid we can't control ourselves or make the right decisions on our own.

Let's suppose you refrained from pre-marital intercourse or drinking alcoholic beverages because of the pressures of your parents or your church. Then you leave home for work or college and find out God doesn't punish you for sin. Some friends encourage drinking and pre-marital sex and you are strongly tempted. All of a sudden you're afraid you can't restrain yourself. Why? Because you have had little experience in self-control. All your controls have been external. Without them you are frightened by your own desires. The student who said, "If I believed all that, I'd really sin it up," was really saying, "If God doesn't punish me, withdraw his acceptance, or make me feel miserable for my sins, I'm afraid I won't be able to keep myself in line."

Even those of us who are not afraid of our own reactions fear that others will lose control without proper external pressure. We have been so used to controlling others we can't trust them to control themselves.

Suppose you were suddenly thrown into a society where there was no direction at all. You were told you could do exactly as you wished without one prohibition. You would immediately become anxious and look for guidelines. You would be afraid of doing the wrong thing and of hurting yourself or someone else. You would want some limits and controls placed on yourself and others.

The same is true in the spiritual realm. Although the Bible gives us guidelines, they are not enough for the insecure person. He cannot trust the internal guidance of the Holy Spirit, so he must seek detailed external rules to relieve his feelings of inadequacy. Legalistic rules fit right into our need for security. They keep us from having to think for ourselves and face the conflicts of decision-making, or they help us manipulate others by doing their thinking.

This search for external controls isn't limited to the person who has had strict parents. Even in permissive homes we find a similar dynamic. No matter how permissive parents are, they still occasionally lose their tempers and punish or threaten their children even though they fail to discipline them physically. This leaves even the products of permissive homes with a similar core of fear and search for security. Others, lacking any parental guidance, start looking to the church for external direction. This makes them, too, susceptible to a set of legalistic standards.

In a similar way, this search for security is a major driving force behind the domineering leader. Although he appears outwardly strong and confident, he inwardly carries a deeply hidden fear of weakness and insecurity. By developing a strong, rigid, dogmatic personality style, he is able to hide his inner feelings and convince himself and others of his strengths.

### *"I'm Helpless"*

Related to the search for security through legalism is the desire also for dependency and approval. Everyone wants to be loved and accepted. But sometimes this need becomes excessive and we go to great lengths to avoid criticism or disapproval. We can become so fearful of rejection that we won't assert ourselves or think for ourselves. This makes us dependent on someone else's standards and content with external rules.

This dependent, compliant personality fits nicely into the congregation of an externally strong and aggressive pastor who is unknowingly trying to cover his own fears by becoming a strong, authoritarian type of leader. The pastor has a need to bolster his ego by being the authority on all sorts of issues. At the same time, the dependent person has a need for a strong authority to follow, and gains a sense of power and approval by aligning himself to the "strong" leader. This is frequently seen in churches and organizations with one "strong" personality as the leader and a large number of disciples following closely behind in thinly-veiled hero worship.

## The Force of Habit

All parents have a set of standards and beliefs they consider "right." Usually our churches and sub-cultures uphold similar values. As we spend fifteen or twenty years in an environment with concrete beliefs, we often adopt its values as our own. The person raised in a racially prejudiced home, and the person who is taught that certain innocent amusements are terrible sin, will often carry these attitudes into adulthood. These habits help program us for the rigidities of legalism and external conformity.

## Seeing Ourselves in Others

Even when we hide our bad attitudes, they continue to stir up trouble and search for an outlet. In an effort to keep them in check, we search for a scapegoat to project the blame on. We often attack in others the sins we unknowingly would like to commit ourselves.

I encountered an extreme example of this in a recent series of counseling sessions. This man was the most effective evangelist in the United States for his entire denomination. He was known for a series of sermons in which he strongly attacked the evils of alcohol, drugs, illicit sex, and other taboos. He traveled throughout the country holding meetings almost every night until his overwhelming schedule forced him to take a rest. Within two weeks of his last sermon he was having an adulterous affair and using drugs! During a counseling session he said pitifully, "As long as I could preach against those things, I was okay. But when I couldn't warn others anymore, I just lost control."

In lesser degrees, many of us project our own unconscious desires and sinful wishes onto others. Somebody who repeatedly emphasizes one or a few taboo behaviors is likely working on his own unconscious problem. Again, legalistic rules cater to this need to project blame on others and deny our own weaknesses.

## The Law Isn't Useless

If legalism has such negative effects, is the law of any value? Shouldn't we throw it out and get on with living under grace? Paul anticipated this question when he asked, "What shall we say then? Is the law sin?" Then he answers this rhetorical question with the reply, "May it never be! On the contrary, I would not have come to know sin except through the law" (Romans 7:7, *NASB*).

### The Law Shows Us Right and Wrong

The law is a revelation of God's righteousness. As such, its purpose is to let us know what is right and what is wrong. Without a revelation of this kind from God, we are left guessing both for ourselves and society. With it, we have a dependable guide to constructive living. God's law lays moral ground rules. We know that even if we are under grace and forgiven, we will suffer natural consequences if we violate God's righteousness. The law is a picture of how our lives can run most beneficially.

### The Law Drives Us to Grace

The law also shows us our moral failures and our total inability to please God apart from Christ. One good reading of the Sermon on the Mount makes this clear. To lust is the same as to commit adultery, to covet is to steal, to be bitter is the same as murder. Every hidden attitude is revealed as sin.

The law threatens us with judgment for not conforming to its right demands. This should bring us to complete frustration. When we see ourselves in the light of God's standards and devoid of the righteousness he demands, we are ready for Christ and grace. In this way the law serves a good purpose—it brings us to Christ and grace where our anxiety can vanish. Paul says, "The law has become our tutor to lead us to Christ, that we may be justified by faith" (Galatians 3:24, *NASB*).

For non-Christians, the law principles of fear and judgment may become an important factor in motivating a turn to Christ, although love appeals more to most people than fear. Some morally rebellious persons need the law to realize God will judge their rebellion. In both cases the law does not rescue anyone, but it drives them to Christ and grace where they can be rescued.

The Christian does not need to be driven to Christ and grace—he is already there. For him to seek God's approval through legalistic principles is not only a hopeless endeavor but the use of God's laws for destructive purposes. It is a gross perversion that stirs vehement New Testament opposition.

## Legalism Is Opposed to Law!

The law is God's program to prove that we are failures on our own. Once we see we are unable to meet his standards, we can turn to Christ to gain acceptance. In contrast to this helpful function of the law, legalism is a human life-style contrived to resist God's attempts to show us we're failures. Legalism tries to demonstrate our goodness. We substitute our keepable rules for God's impossible standards. We substitute observable externals for the hidden purity of heart he demands, and we cling to a human righteousness in place of unattainable divine holiness. Legalism is not the Christian way of life. It is actually a neatly disguised form of rebellion. God has something far better for us, and those who submit to the grace of Christ will want to leave legalism far behind.

# 12

# What Do You Do When You Blow It?

A student named Jim grew up in a conservative home in rural Nebraska. Coming to the West Coast on an athletic scholarship, he soon found himself in the midst of a group of "swingers." Although he was a Christian, it wasn't long before he was into drugs and living with a girl. About this time I ran into him. He was miserable and wanted help. He wanted to "get back into God's good graces" but didn't know how to do it.

Jack was a business executive. He, too, was a Christian and considered himself a "family man." He also taught a Sunday school class at his local church. During a lengthy business trip overseas Jack struck up a conversation with an attractive woman, recently divorced. They were both lonely and you can guess what happened before the night was over. Because Jack was a personal friend, he sought me out for help. He asked questions like, "How can I face my family?" "How can I ever feel worthy of sharing my faith in Christ again?" and "Should I keep teaching my Sunday school class?"

Jim and Jack faced the identical problem. How were they to react now that they had fallen into overt sin? All of us, of course, have similar problems. while we may not get involved with drugs or illicit sex, we do "blow it" from time to time, and we feel guilty after we engage in some obvious sort of sin or some "lesser" evils like gossip, envy, or hostile remarks to our mates. And, lamentably, we often feel guilty for things that aren't even mentioned in the Bible.

We have seen how Christ died to free us totally from guilt. But now we need to see how this works. We want to lay open God's plan for guilt-free living and a positive Christian life.

## Who Says You Blew It?

The first question we should ask ourselves when we feel a tinge of guilt is, "*Did I really blow it?*" In other words, we want to determine if we really did something wrong or if we only violated the childish standards of our ideal self—our inner parent. Most of us feel guilty over a number of things God doesn't consider sin.

I often encounter college students whose parents are absolutely determined their children get their college degrees. Sometime during their college years the students wake up to the fact they don't want to be in college. They would prefer to marry or enter a vocation that doesn't require college education. Yet as soon as they consider "dropping out" they start feeling guilty. They're afraid they're letting their parents down. Later if they do drop out, they may repeatedly be haunted by the thought that they made the wrong decision. When a girl in this situation marries, she often starts resenting her husband for "depriving her of an education or profession."

In similar ways, we all feel guilty over some less-than-perfect ideals. Some men feel guilty if they aren't working all the time. Some women feel guilty if their homes aren't spotless. Some of us feel guilty if we have nice things, and others feel guilty if we don't. Still others feel guilty if they don't say yes to every request to serve in their church or social organization.

But the Bible doesn't say every American should get a college degree, have a spotless home, teach a Sunday school class or work sixteen hours a day. Many people who battle guilt are not doing wrong; they are condemning themselves for failing to live up to their ideal self—the borrowed standards of their parents or society.

We shouldn't assume that all values that have been fed into our ideal self are correct. As remnants of our childish past, the values of our ideal self may be horribly fallible. Some people's ideals literally let them get away with murder. They can have a round of sexual affairs without a trace of conscious guilt, while others feel slightly guilty if they buy a tube of toothpaste that was advertised to have "sex appeal."

As adults we must modify our ideal selves in accordance with the Bible and good common sense. "Let your conscience be your guide" is not in the Bible! Our consciences are fallible.

## What's the Real Problem?

When we are feeling guilty, we also need to *look for the real problem.* Sometimes we feel guilty over *symptoms* and don't recognize the *hidden problem.* When this happens, we may confess the symptoms and try to clear up our guilt over them but leave the root problem there to do its damage. When we repeatedly confess a sin and still feel guilty, this is usually what's happening. We are praying over the wrong sin. This also happens when we make the same mistakes over and over again. The reason we don't change is that we're fighting the wrong problem.

### Family Warfare

A friend of mine was constantly irritated with his wife. He felt a mild hostility toward her every time she made suggestions, even though they might be good. As we talked, he discovered that his oversensitivity was just the tip of a great iceberg of hostility. Underneath, he had deep-seated feelings of resentment. He felt his wife was more successful than he and that she had a "superior" attitude. He also found out he had buried resentments toward his mother. When his wife did anything remotely like his mother, he reacted with hostility. As he got this out and looked at it, he faced his responsibility in the matter. By taking constructive steps to alter his reactions, the constant irritation gradually disappeared.

### Sex Habits

A young adult I was counseling complained about habitual masturbation. Although he repeatedly confessed his actions, he continued to feel guilty and repeated his habit in a day or two. Over a period of several weeks we talked about his problem. Gradually a clearer picture started to emerge. From early childhood he'd felt inferior and inadequate as a male. Although he was athletic and good looking as a teenager, he was shy around girls and dated very little.

He began to resent girls because he didn't think they liked him or wanted to date. During this time he began to masturbate. His self stimulation became a regular escape. Since he felt too inadequate to have a real relationship with a girl, he gave in to his habit and engaged in a fantasy relationship.

He imagined he was sexually conquering a variety of female acquaintances. This allowed him to express his anger toward women, avoid his feelings of inadequacy in their presence, gain a temporary feeling of masculinity, and discharge his sexual tensions. Although he felt guilty over masturbation, that was just a symptom. His real problem was how he felt about himself and his relationships with the opposite sex. Dealing with symptoms is usually not enough. We must learn to face our inner problems.

### Who Is Your Accuser?

Once we've seen our real sin in its true light, we need to ask ourselves, "*Where is my feeling of guilt coming from?*" Remember what we said about the "punitive-self"—those internalized disciplinary attitudes of our parents? When we violate our standards, this punitive-self immediately goes to work. It mentally inflicts some kind of punishment just as our parents did years before. It may say, "You're bad," "You're a failure," "You're a hypocrite," "You deserve to be punished," or "How could God love you?" Again, we assume this nagging conscience is the voice of God. We think God is "convicting" us of our sin.

In reality, these guilt feelings aren't the voice of God at all. God never makes a Christian feel psychological guilt. These feelings are always products of our early family training. The devil gladly takes advantage of them and compounds our guilt. He helps us think, "You're bad"; "How can you claim to be a Christian?" or "What a hypocrite you are."

In this way the devil pulls off one of his biggest tricks. For centuries Christians have thought guilt feelings were the voice of God. In reality, they result from the devil using our inner punitive attitudes to frustrate and defeat us. The Bible makes this very clear. It says that Satan is the "accuser of the brethren" and that Jesus is our "advocate." (Revelation 12:10; 1 John 2:1, 2, *NASB*). How deceived we have been to think God is speaking to us when we feel guilty and think the devil is lulling us into complacency when we feel innocent. Just the opposite is true.

The great reformer Martin Luther spotted this in his own life. When he felt the law accusing him, he would say: "Mr. Law, go ahead and accuse me as much as you like, I know I have committed many sins, and I continue to sin daily. But that doesn't bother me. You have got to shout louder, Mr. Law. I am deaf, you know. Talk as much as you like, I am dead to you. . . . My conscience is a lady and a queen, and has nothing to do with the likes of you, because my conscience lives to Christ under another law, a new and better law, the law of grace."[1]

Here was the spirit of the Reformation. After centuries of oppressive legalism, Luther and other reformers struck a blow for freedom. They loudly proclaimed the grace of God that frees men from bondage to their guilt. How badly our generation needs another dose of this liberating truth. As Paul so plainly put it, "Who will bring a charge against God's elect? God is the one who justifies; who is the one who condemns? Christ Jesus is he who died, yes, rather who was raised, who is at the right hand of God, who also intercedes for us" (Romans 8:33, 34, *NASB*). At another point he says: "There is therefore now no condemnation to them that are in Christ Jesus" (Romans 8:1, *NASB*).

When guilt comes we need to clearly set this truth in mind. Guilt feelings—as distinct from constructive sorrow— are the devil's tool. They do not come from God. Christ has paid the penalty of sin and set us forever free from the curse of law and guilt.

## God's Alternative to Psychological Guilt

Once we have recognized the harmful effects of guilt feelings we are free to turn to a constructive alternative. The Bible doesn't say we are free from guilt so we can "sin it up." Instead, it says we are free from guilt so we can learn to fulfill our lives and develop inner character. We call the vehicle for this change "constructive sorrow."

Paul carefully notes the difference between psychological guilt and this helpful reaction in Second Corinthians 7:8-10. He writes: "For though I caused you sorrow by my letter, I do not regret it, though I did regret it; for I see that that letter caused you sorrow, though only for a while. I now rejoice, not that you were made sorrowful, but that you were made sorrowful to the point of repentance; for you were made sorrowful according to the will of God, in order that you might not suffer loss in anything through us. For the sorrow that is according to the will of God produces a repentance without regret, leading to salvation; but the sorrow of the world produces death" (*NASB*).

Paul speaks of the "sorrow of the world" (literally "grief") and the "sorrow according to the will of God." He says the sorrow of the world produces nothing positive. It leads only to death. In contrast, the "sorrow according to the will of God" is helpful. It leads to repentance.

### Turn About Is Fair Play

The Greek word for repentance actually means to "change your mind." For example, on the day of Pentecost Peter concluded his famous sermon by telling his Jewish audience to "repent and let each of you be baptized in the name of Jesus Christ" (Acts 2:38, *NASB*). Two months earlier, this same Jewish audience had approved of the crucifixion of Jesus. Peter challenges them to "change their minds" about Jesus and his crucifixion, and believe in him instead.

Repentance implies a decision of the will and should lead to changed behavior. In Second Corinthians 7:11 Paul says godly sorrow led to repentance that led to increased earnestness, respect, and zeal. *Psychological guilt produces self-inflicted misery. Constructive sorrow produces a positive change of behavior.* Once the change in behavior comes, constructive sorrow vanishes. Its purpose is accomplished.

### Conviction

I knew of a man who had left his wife and was a heavy drinker. An acquaintance of his said to me, "I hope God convicts him, makes him miserable, and won't let him have a good night's sleep until he straightens out." Many people have the same view of conviction. They think "conviction" is "God making us miserable." But this isn't so. We may be miserable because of sin, but not because God is making us so.

God is consistent. He doesn't tell us we are significant, forgiven, and disciplined only in love, then whisper in our ears, "You are a scoundrel; I will punish you. I will pay you back until you repent." God cannot contradict himself! He doesn't present one message in the Bible and an opposite message by his "convicting Holy Spirit." Conviction simply means that God is clearly showing us our sins and admonishing us to change.

The Bible clearly pictures the way God approaches erring Christians. For example, the Apostle Paul was inspired by God to correct the sinning Corinthian Christians. They were still entrapped in many of their pagan ways. Church members were divided against each other, suing each other, committing incest, and getting drunk at the communion service!

In the first chapter of his first letter to the Corinthians, Paul reminds them of their high and holy calling as Christians. Then he proceeds to rebuke them in love for their faults and show them how ridiculous their behavior is. He leaves no stone unturned in correcing them, but he does it in obvious love and convern, without scathing denunciations.

In the same way, as a firm but loving parent, God comes to us and convicts us of our sin. The natural reaction it produces is just what Paul got from the Corinthians—constructive sorrow. Unfortunately, we twist God's convicting of us into a condemnation of us, then respond with the various guilt games described in Chapter Four.

### Guilt is Selfish

Psychological guilt and constructive sorrow are very different feelings. Psychological guilt is largely self-centered. Its real concern is not, "What have I done to others and how can I correct the harm I have done them?" Instead, it focuses on: "What a failure *I* am"; "What will everyone think of *me*?" or "*I* am no good." Adam and Eve apparently didn't have the slightest concern that they had plunged the world into rebellion and thrown a monkey wrench into God's plan for the universe. They were just afraid they would be punished—one form of guilt.

Guilt focuses largely on our past failures, our sense of wrongdoing, and our feelings of deserving punishment. In short, it looks largely at ourselves and at our failures. Constructive sorrow focuses more on the persons we have injured. It is a very deep feeling but is not as concerned with our own failures as it is the damage done to others.

### Don't Cry Over Spilt Coffee!

Let me illustrate this further. Let's say the two of us are chatting over coffee. Reaching for the sugar, I accidentally knock your coffee in your lap. A typical guilt reaction would be, "How stupid of me. I should have known better.

Look at the mess I've made. I'm sorry." In my mind (if not verbally) I might continue to berate myself and feel like a social idiot. The focus here is on myself and my misdeeds.

Constructive sorrow is very different. I might say something like, "I'm so sorry. Here are some napkins. I'll get the table cleaned up." And later I might offer to pay the cleaning bill.

|  | PSYCHOLOGICAL GUILT | CONSTRUCTIVE SORROW |
|---|---|---|
| *Person in primary focus* | Your self | God or others |
| *Attitudes or actions in Primary Focus* | Past misdeeds | Damage done to others or our future correct deeds |
| *Motivation for change (if any)* | To avoid feeling bad (guilt feelings) | To help others, to promote our growth, or to do God's will (love feelings) |
| *Attitude toward ourself* | Anger and frustration | Love and respect combined with concern |
| *Result* | a) External change (for improper motivations)<br>b) Stagnation due to paralyzing effect of guilt<br>c) Further rebellion | Repentance and change based on an attitude of love and mutual respect |

Notice the difference? In the first instance the focus was on myself and my failures. It hardly seemed important that I'd spilled coffee on your clothes. I was more concerned with my own mistake and embarrassment. Even if I'd offered to pay your cleaning bill, I probably would have done it to relieve my guilt. In the second instance you were my main concern. I didn't keep focusing on my failure. And I didn't keep verbally attacking myself. I immediately tried to help. The accompanying chart helps clarify these differences.

## The Continuing Guilt Battle

Unfortunately, we sometimes find it hard to tell the difference between guilt feelings and constructive sorrow. As sinful, self-centered people, our first concern is usually for ourselves. We are more concerned about being caught and punished than we are about the harm we've done to others. Only as we accept God's forgiveness and turn our focus to others can we move toward the deep biblical feeling of constructive sorrow.

An important aspect of this process is what the Bible calls confession. This is so vital, yet so often misunderstood, that we will devote the whole next chapter to it.

FOOTNOTES

1. Luther, Martin: *Commentary on the Epistle to the Galatians* (Zondervan, 1949), p. 175.

# 13

# True Confessions

During a series of meetings with a group of pastors, a minister came and asked to see me privately. During our talk together he said, "I have something that's bothered me for years. When I was in seminary I cheated on my final Greek exam. When I took the test I accidentally omitted one section of translation. Since I usually did well in class, my professor called me at home to see what happened. I was shocked and told him I didn't realize I had left it out. Since he trusted me a lot, he said, 'I'll let you translate that passage to me over the phone now.' I told him all right, excused myself for a moment, and got both my Greek New Testament and an English translation. Then I translated it over the phone. But I was actually reading from the English. I got an A in the class and graduated from seminary with honors, but I can't look that professor in the eye to this day. Every time I think about it, I feel like a hypocrite. I've prayed and prayed about it, but nothing seems to change."

After talking over the situation, I suggested the only way to resolve the problem would be to telephone his professor and confess his cheating. He struggled with this for some minutes and finally said, "I just can't do it. What would he think of me?"

I've never seen this pastor since, but I imagine he's still

haunted by his guilt. His refusal to confess his cheating left him a victim of self-punishment.

### *"You've Lifted A Million Pounds Off My Back!"*

On another occasion I talked with a college freshman who had been sexually pure all of her life. She was committed to her Christian faith and had struck up a romance with one of the leaders of the Christian student group on campus. One night they lost control and went to bed together. They felt too guilty to see each other any more and broke off the relationship. But her guilt feelings continued to plague her. Finally she came to me and unloaded the story. After talking over her feelings and behavior I assured her of God's forgiveness. Then she looked at me and said, "I feel like you've lifted a million pounds off my back."

### *The Fear of Being Known*

These real-life illustrations point out a crucial ingredient of positive spiritual and emotional health. If we hide our sins and problems, we will be plagued with various forms of guilt. But if we acknowledge our offenses and get them out in the open, we can feel forgiven and experience peace and reconciliation.

This sounds good, but it isn't always easy! No one likes to admit his mistakes. We think, "If people knew what I'd done, they wouldn't respect me," or, "If they knew, they might get angry," or, "If they knew, they might not like me any more." Each of these thoughts reflects our feelings of psychological guilt. Translated into our present context, they are ways of saying, "I'm afraid I will lose self-esteem, get punished, or be rejected if I admit my sins."

Since no one wants this to happen, we hide our problems. But what goes on inside? Even though nobody knows what we've done, we keep thinking, "*If* they knew, they wouldn't like me." In other words, even when we hide our faults, we keep feeling guilty.

Sometimes it gets worse. We tell a lie or two to cover up our misbehavior or we put on a false front of goodness. This additional dishonesty builds more guilt.

Each time this happens we weave a thicker web of dishonesty and guilt. What started as an attempt to avoid a loss of self-esteem, punishment, or rejection becomes a generator of these feelings. Added to this is a self-imposed isolation; we feel we can't be honest with others, so we keep our distance. This causes loneliness to come in on top of everything else.

### How David Was Done In

The Bible presents a graphic illustration of this in the life of King David. As he was walking around the roof of his house one day, David saw a beautiful woman named Bathsheba taking her evening bath. He sent for her, committed adultery, and got her pregnant. At this point David knew he had sinned, but he didn't want anyone else to know, so he arranged to have the woman's husband put in the front lines of a battle where he would be killed. To hide one sin (adultery) David committed another (murder).

For most of a year David hid those sins. Here's how he describes that year: "When I kept silent about my sin, my body wasted away through my groaning all day long. For day and night thy hand was heavy upon me; my vitality was drained away as with the fever heat of summer" (Psalm 32:3, 4, *NASB*).

David was depressed, physically run down, and out of touch with God. In short, he felt extremely guilty. Finally, David came to his senses and admitted his sins to God (who, of course, knew them all the time!). He prayed:

"Be gracious to me, O God, according to thy lovingkindness; according to the greatness of thy compassion blot out my transgressions. Wash me thoroughly from my iniquity, and cleanse me from my sin. For I know my transgressions, and my sin is ever before me. Against thee, thee only, I have sinned, and done what is evil in thy sight" (Psalm 51:1-4, *NASB*).

Here David goes through a deep confession experience. For months he has feared God's punishment and rejection. He has felt so guilty he developed psychosomatic symptoms. He has suffered an intense loss of self-esteem. And he even feared the Lord would withdraw his Holy Spirit from him.[1]

David's full confession, recorded in Psalm 51, reflects both psychological guilt and constructive sorrow. If David had immediately repented over his sins, he would have avoided much psychological guilt. But the long delay, compounded by further deception, loneliness, and David's own psychological makeup programmed him for destructive guilt. David says God's hand of conviction was "heavy upon me." But his response of illness, depression, and further delay certainly did not represent constructive sorrow—they were his self-imposed destructive feelings.

This illustrates the importance of distinguishing God's conviction from our response to God's conviction. God's convicting work tells us we are wrong, where we are wrong, and what we should do about it. We may respond to this conviction with feelings of self-hatred, fear and misery—the elements of psychological guilt. We can respond with hostility, or indifference. Or we can respond with constructive sorrow. The miserable feelings of psychological guilt that David experienced weren't sent to him by God. They were caused by his own self-punitive attitudes and his long months of living in deceit. Psychological guilt helped keep David in spiritual paralysis for a year! Constructive sorrow brought him immediate repentance and release.

## Confession and Catharsis

The same is true of all of us. When we wrong someone or commit a sin, our guilt feelings usually begin to grow. We start to think (usually wrongly) that people will reject us or be angry with us. The longer we hide it, the more guilty we feel and the more fearful we become. Finally, when we do confess our faults, we suddenly find out we really are forgiven and we find out the fears of others' anger were unjustified. If we had only confessed our faults sooner we wouldn't have had to suffer the pangs of self-inflicted guilt. Confession helps us keep clear of guilt and leads us naturally to constructive sorrow. Confession is God's way of avoiding the guilt trap.

Realizing our universal tendency to hide our inner problems, the Bible tells us we should acknowledge our sins to ourselves, others (when appropriate), and to God. Consider the following typical examples:

"He who conceals his transgressions will not prosper, but he who confesses and forsakes them will find compassion" (Proverbs 28:13, *NASB*).

"If we confess our sins, he is faithful and righteous to forgive us our sins and to cleanse us from all unrighteousness" (1 John 1:9, *NASB*).

"Therefore, confess your sins to one another, and pray for one another, so that you may be healed. The effective prayer of a righteous man can accomplish much" (James 5:16, *NASB*).

These passages tell us that confession is essential both to a healthy relationship with God and to our personal adjustment. There is a positive cathartic effect by confession of our sins to God and others. It helps us knock the lid off our repressions and get God's perspective on our lives. Instead of hiding our failings for fear of punishment and rejection, we get them out in the open so they can be dealt with. This confession is crucial to our personal growth.

## Abuses of Confession

### Confession as Self-Punishment

As important as it is, confession can be greatly misunderstood and misused. Some people, for example, use confession as a form of self-punishment. Failing to realize emotionally that Christ has delivered them from condemnation, they morbidly introspect and constantly condemn themselves. Rather than applying God's forgiveness to their sins, their confession only keeps them feeling guilty and worthless. Their prayers focus largely on their sins and sense of worthlessness and they use confession to condemn themselves rather than to lay hold of their forgiveness. This reinforces their guilt and negative self-image.

### Skin-Deep Confession

Others use confession like a magic ritual. They rattle off confessions of sin like a routine prayer of thanks before dinner. They are like the child caught with his hand in the cookie jar who says, "I'm sorry. Don't spank me." He isn't sorry he did it. He's only sorry he got caught and wants to use the magic words to ward off punishment or rejection.

Sometimes we do the same with God. When we remember a sin we think, "Oh-oh, I'd better confess it or God will get upset with me and I'll lose out." Then we "confess" our sin and imagine we're back in a right relationship with God. But we have just waved confession over our fault like a magic wand and hoped everything will be all right. In reality, confession has little value unless we honestly face our failure and begin to feel some genuine repentance. The goal of confession is nothing short of healthy behavior change. People who constantly confess but never change need to come more to grips with their real problems.

### Confession and Forgiveness

We saw in chapter eight that God never even temporarily rejects those who have become Christians. Although we may feel barriers between ourselves and God, God has no barrier. Any feeling of being alienated from God arises from our own fears rather than from the objective facts of God's attitude toward us. God's attitude toward us is always constant. Even confession and repentance can't change his attitude toward us. Technically speaking, Christians are not forgiven because we confess our sins. The basis on which God forgives us is our acceptance of Christ. By appropriating his atonement we receive divine forgiveness. The purpose of confession is to help us agree with God's evaluation of our condition and experience God's forgiveness. David was forgiven through his faith, but his confession helped him immensely to feel forgiven. It helped him appropriate a forgiveness he already had.

### *The Old and the New*

Though God has always granted eternal and final forgiveness to all true believers, the New Testament letters shed light on the subject of forgiveness that was not present in the Old.

Old Testament believers did not have as clear a revelation of the finality and permanence of God's forgiveness as we do. For them, forgiveness was tied to a system of animal sacrifices. They made repeated sacrifices and obtained repeated forgiveness. The one final forgiveness which would wipe away the necessity for the sacrificial system was unclear. They only imperfectly realized that the animal sacrifice pictured ahead of time the sacrifice of Christ on which final forgiveness is based.

After the death of Christ, the Bible teaches that the old system of repeated sacrifices to obtain temporary forgiveness was abolished. The Letter to the Hebrews contrasts the two systems. First the old: "And every priest stands daily ministering and offering time after time the same sacrifices, which can never take away sins . . . "; then the new: " . . . but he [Christ], having offered one sacrifice for sins for all time, sat down at the right hand of God" (Hebrews 10:11, 12, *NASB*). Then the writer adds: "Now where there is forgiveness of these things, there is no longer any offering for sin" (10:18, *NASB*). He clearly states that now that final forgiveness is here, the old system with its sacrifices and offerings is abolished.

The New Testament clearly reveals what had not been so clear before Christ's death—that all sins, past, present, and future are forgiven once and for all through the atonement of Christ. When we accept Christ, we obtain all the forgiveness we ever need.

This is easy to say, but difficult to experience. Our years of experience with people have programmed us to think we need a new forgiveness for each offense. Sensitive people, especially, tend to feel they lose their forgiveness each time they commit another sin. Even though they may intellectually know God has forgiven all their sins, they cannot emotionally believe it. Some even go to the extent of convincing themselves they have committed the unforgiveable sin and are now beyond hope.[2]

### "We're All Guilty of the Two Worst Sins"

One way to understand how it is that we are always acceptable to a perfect God is to get his view of sin. In chapter eight we saw that there is never one moment any of us are without some sin—either conscious or unconscious, large or small. None of us, for example, fulfill what Christ said were the two greatest commandments. Jesus said we were to love God with all our strength and to love our neighbors as ourselves (Mark 12:28-31). Failing to love like this is the worst thing we can do, for it violates Christ's greatest commandment. Yet none of us ever lives with this perfect love. Although we can approach it in varying degrees, we never get completely there. Since we don't, how can we maintain our acceptance with God?

Because God's holy nature demands perfect righteousness, he can't fellowship with us at all unless we have it. The solution to the dilemma lies, of course, in the fact that all Christians do have all of Christ's righteousness imputed to them. This is why Paul could write, "So now, since we have been made right in God's sight by faith in his promises, we can have real peace with him because of what Jesus Christ our Lord has done for us" (Romans 5:1, *TLB*). Also: "Adam's sin brought punishment to all, but Christ's righteousness makes men right with God, so that they can live. Adam caused many to be sinners because he disobeyed God, and Christ caused many to be made acceptable to God because he obeyed" (Romans 5:18, 19, *TLB*). This is the dynamic that constantly keeps us in fellowship with God.

Seen in this light, the primary purpose of confession is to help us get in agreement with God's view of our life situation. For Christians, an open confession or acknowledging of our sins is the happiest way of life. By admitting our sins to God we open ourselves up to his correction and we re-experience the sense of forgiveness we often lose when we sin. This keeps us open and receptive to God's uninterrupted flow of love and keeps us from getting entangled in the snares of guilt emotions.

As we saw in Chapters Seven and Nine, this doesn't mean God is passive when we sin. He does instruct, convict, and discipline. Sometimes the discipline comes through the natural bad consequences of our behavior. On other occasions God clearly intervenes to lovingly discipline us. This can include anything from the loving rebuke of a Christian friend to serious financial or physical hardships. The more we confess and repent of our sins on our own, the less God has to discipline us. Paul wisely writes, "If we evaluated ourselves rightly, we should not be disciplined. But when we are disciplined, we are corrected by the Lord in order that we may not be condemned along with the world" (1 Corinthians 11:31, 32, *paraphrased*).

We should also remember that God disciplines all of us through many life experiences. Since we are all in various stages of maturity, he deals with us in different ways. It seems obvious, however, that blatant, unrepented sins may bring more serious forms of discipline. But how much conviction, natural bad consequences, discipline, and other related problems come to us and over what issues is really up to God. He usually works on one or a few areas of our lives at a time because we are slow to learn. When we have matured in those areas, he then reveals new places we need to grow and starts helping us in them.

## Avoid It Like the Plague

Unrepented, unconfessed sin is never worth it. It tends to affect vast areas of our lives. Psalm 66:18, 19 says, "If I regard wickedness in my heart, the Lord will not hear . . . " (*NASB*). In a similar vein James 4:3 says, "You ask and do not receive, because you ask with wrong motives, so that you may spend it on your pleasures" (*NASB*). These verses don't mean that God doesn't listen when we pray or turns his back on us. As we have seen, if sin kept God from hearing us, he could never listen since we're never totally free of sin. But they do teach that sin in our lives often makes us pray wrongly or selfishly. God won't give us the answer we want if we are praying for the wrong thing. In this way unconfessed and unrepented sin keeps us from accurately tuning in on God's will for us, and can also harm that area of our life.

Though God forgives all of our sins and won't punish us for them, we can't treat sin lightly and think unrepented sins don't matter. They can make a great difference in this world: the difference between happiness and misery, guilt and freedom, and success and failure.

FOOTNOTES

1. Although in Old Testament times God sent the Holy Spirit to believers for certain tasks and could withdraw him, this is not true after Christ's death. All Christians are given the Holy Spirit to indwell them forever and need not fear this rejection. John 14:16 says, "And I will ask the Father, and he will give you another Helper, that he may be with you forever" (*NASB*).

2. The Bible does mention an unpardonable sin in Matthew 12:31 32, Mark 3:28-30 and Luke 12:10. First John 5:16 and Hebrews 6 and 10 may refer to the same sin. This sin, however, involves rejecting the Holy Spirit's teaching about the person and work of Christ. Since Christians have already accepted Christ's person and work, it is impossible for them to commit this unpardonable sin.

# 14

# Decisions, Decisions!

Years ago I had an unforgettable experience. A friend telephoned me one evening and told me he was God. He had been severely disturbed for several days, and that day suffered a complete emotional breakdown, fleeing into a delusional world.

As I tried to help him and his family put the pieces back together, I discovered what had precipitated the breakdown. He had to make a number of important decisions that were going to affect his life for many years. The pressures of these decisions were too much and he broke under the strain. Obviously the decisions weren't the original cause of his problems. He had always lacked confidence and been sensitive to pressure. But the added weight of heavy decisions became the straw that broke the camel's back.

Making our own decisions and running our own lives is serious business. Occasionally it creates some anxiety in all of us. Don't we often wonder just what we ought to do? And aren't we sometimes afraid we'll make the wrong decisions? Not only with major decisions, but in the innumerable decisions of everyday life we think, "On what basis am I to make decisions," or "What is right or wrong?"

To some fearful people the answer is quite simple. If at all possible they let others decide for them. They are drawn to overly-structured churches and organizations. They want others to tell them how a good Christian should act or think or feel, so they don't have to think for themselves. As long as they obey other people's rules they can pat themselves on the back and say, "Well done." If things go wrong, they aren't to blame because they played by the rules. They did their part.

Others go to the opposite extreme. They think, "Now that I'm free I'll do just what I want. I won't listen to anyone." Both of these approaches can bring disaster. While there are times we should follow instructions without question, there are other times we should make our own decisions. Freedom is like a river between two banks. One bank is anarchy and moral license. The other is religious legalism and externalism. The river of freedom should always stay between these two. If we go to the side of license and rebellion we become enslaved to our impulses. If we reach for the security of legalism, we become entrapped in an opposite type of slavery. Either side is equally as damaging. The Bible gives us wise counsel so we can avoid these extremes and enjoy personal inner freedom that leads to responsible interactions with ourselves and others.

## Three Ways To Go

The Bible defines three categories of behavior: (1) some behavior is clearly wrong, (2) some behavior is clearly right and good, (3) some behavior in and of itself is neutral, but may become right or wrong, depending on the situation.

The first two categories are rather easily understood. We are not to murder (Exodus 20:13), commit adultery (verse 14), steal (verse 15), lie (verse 15), be greedy (verse 16) or spread unnecessary strife among friends (Proverbs 6:19). Many other attitudes and actions would come under this category of wrong behavior.

In contrast, we are expected to share our Christian faith (Matthew 28:19, 20), pray (1 Thessalonians 5:17), love even our enemies (Matthew 5:43), study the Bible (2 Timothy 2:15), be thankful (1 Thessalonians 5:18), and give our attention to what is honorable and good (Philippians 4:8).

As with the list of named sins, the Bible gives quite a number of these positive attitudes and actions.

Between these two categories lies behavior neither specifically forbidden nor specifically endorsed, but acceptable for some people at some times and unacceptable for other people at other times. This third category isn't a gray area where things are slightly bad, but not bad enough to merit the label "sin." Nor is it an area where our choices make no difference. Instead, the activities in this third category become black or white—right or wrong—in different situations based on the application of some specific biblical principles.

## Doubtful Things in Corinth

Paul's first letter to the Corinthians spells out the principles which help us decide in the third area. The city of Corinth, like most ancient cities, overflowed with pagan temples of worship. Part of the worship in these temples included sexual immorality with temple prostitutes. Another part often included a wild, drunken feast or banquet in the temple where food was offered to temple idols. This posed serious questions to the Christians of that day. The temple was a central part of their culture. Should they keep attending the temple feasts? Should they eat meat offered to idols and afterward sold at the temple market? Or should they stay entirely out of that scene?

### Flirting With the Devil

Some Corinthians continued going to the idol banquets after they became Christians. They reasoned, "Why not have a meal with my friends? If they worship idols and get drunk, that's all right. I don't have to."

Paul says this is wrong. He says the idolatry and sexual permissiveness of the pagan parties might be too much for the Christian to withstand. He wrote, "Therefore let him who thinks he stands take heed lest he fall" (1 Corinthians 10:12, *NASB*). Here Paul clearly sets forth an example of prohibited behavior. Some Corinthians were flirting with sin.

No clever reasoning could justify getting this close to idolatry and immorality. They were in danger of turning liberty into license.

### The First Century Meat Crisis

After the idol banquets were over, the leftover food was often sold in the Corinthian market place. If you were doing your weekly shopping you could buy a juicy steak, take it home and eat it without being in the atmosphere of idolatry. But would this be all right? Some Corinthians evidently felt this, too, was sin. They said that to even eat the meat in the privacy of your home was participating in idolatry. They were getting like the Pharisees and starting to set up little rules. Paul said this was wrong. He wrote: "Eat anything that is sold in the meat market, without asking questions for conscience' sake; for the earth is the Lord's and everything that is in it" (1 Corinthians 10:25, 26, *NASB*).

In another place Paul said: "I know and am convinced in the Lord Jesus that nothing is unclean in itself" (Romans 14:14, *NASB*). Here Paul sets forth a *principle of liberty*. He says it's perfectly all right to eat meat that has been offered to idols. As a matter of fact, Paul's teaching is that anything not specifically forbidden in the Bible may be done. He says "nothing is unclean of itself." What the Bible does not condemn we are free to do if we so desire. We must avoid interpreting the Bible too narrowly and getting picky about every little detail. We have great freedom!

### Captives of the "Tube"

But Paul didn't stop there. He went on to say, "All things are lawful, but not all things are profitable" (1 Corinthians 10:23, *NASB*). Here he taught that although we are free to engage in certain behaviors, if we find they don't help us we should refrain. This is the *principle of expediency or helpfulness.*

Early in our marriage my wife and I had a good example of this principle. We both spent a good deal of time watching television—newscasts, spy programs, medical dramas, and Monday night football. Nothing about these programs was innately wrong, but we spent too much time in front of "the tube." We weren't communicating with each other or our children as we could have.

One day our son, then aged two, got behind the back panel of our television and spread whipped cream throughout the inner workings of the set. Whipped cream, electronic tubes, and television wiring didn't mix. Our television was out of order!

Being pressed financially, we decided not to fix the set. After a couple of weeks we began to notice a change in atmosphere. The house was quieter, we were talking more, and our family was drawing closer together. We realized that too much television had been bad for us! Some television is constructive, some is relaxing, and some is even inspirational. But in *our* family, at *that* time, it was wrong.

After a year or so of "blackout" we invested in a low-priced portable set. This would let the children watch some programs and also allow us to keep up with world affairs and see a few constructive programs. We hoped we had learned our lesson. And basically we had. While we occasionally slip into our old pattern, we usually watch only on occasion and are no longer TV addicts!

This is what Paul meant by the principle of expediency. Many things are intrinsically neutral (or even good), but when abused or substituted for higher virtues they become hindrances to our growth.

### Situation Ethics in the Bible?

But these weren't the only questions facing the Corinthian church. Suppose a non-Christian invited you to his house for dinner and served you food offered to idols. What are you to do? Paul begins by saying, "Eat anything that is sold in the meat market, without asking questions for conscience' sake" (1 Corinthians 10:25, *NASB*). In other words, if your neighbor serves you a big juicy T-bone steak, even though it was left over from an idol-worshipping banquet, Paul says "Live it up—enjoy your steak."

But suppose your non-Christian host or a weak, uninstructed Christian guest says, "This meat has been offered to idols." Then what do you do? Paul says, " . . . if someone warns you that this meat has been offered to idols, don't eat it for the sake of the man who told you, and of his conscience" (1 Corinthians 10:28, *TLB*). If you eat it he might think you, too, worship his false gods. That will confuse him when you talk to him about the One True God.

Then Paul says: "But why, you may ask, must I be guided and limited by what someone else thinks? If I can thank God for the food and enjoy it, why let someone spoil everything just because he thinks I am wrong? Well, I'll tell you why. It is because you must do everything for the glory of God, even your eating and drinking. So don't be a stumblingblock to anyone, whether they are Jews or Gentiles or Christians. That is the plan I follow, too. I try to please everyone in everything I do, not doing what I like or what is best for me, but what is best for them, so that they may be saved" (10:29b-33, *TLB*). Paul emphasizes here a *principle of love and consideration for others.*

Here is one place in the Bible where we have a valid "situation ethic." I might do opposite things because of the situation, yet not be contradicting myself nor disobeying God. When Paul was with Jews, he ate only kosher food. He didn't bring along his own ham sandwiches to show them he was "free." When he was with Gentiles, on the other hand, he didn't stick to kosher food rules. He flexed.

At this point we often make a mistake. Knowing that certain forms of dress, entertainment, food, and drink will always bother someone somewhere, we may say, "I should never do any of these things just to be on the safe side." We make a universal rule where one does not exist. This only leads to legalism. Actually, Paul's advice is "When you are around the people it will bother, don't do it. When you're not, it's OK." Of course, the immature person insists he should have his freedom no matter what others think. This is pure selfishness, and just as bad an evil in the opposite direction.

I knew a minister who, at a wedding celebration, was invited to toast the bride and groom with a glass of champagne. Most of the people at the celebration drank and had no scruples about it. Since he knew drinking a glass of champagne was not innately sinful, he gladly toasted with them. On the other hand, when he was at another wedding reception where many were teatotalers and would have been offended by his taking a drink, he drank punch. He did the opposite on separate occasions, not for his own sake, but the sake of others.

### Summing Up

We can summarize Paul's teachings briefly. He says that under grace:

(1) we are free to do anything the Bible doesn't forbid.

(2) we shouldn't do anything forbidden in the Bible—that only causes trouble for ourselves and others.

(3) we should refrain from some perfectly legitimate things if they would cause unnecessary problems for another Christian or a non-Christian.

(4) we shouldn't continue in our activity that could become a useless or destructive habit.

## First Century Group Therapy

But these principles are only one side of the coin. We need more than mental knowledge of the Bible to make the right decisions and lead good lives. We also need human interaction. God created us as social and emotional beings and wants us to help each other grow. Though knowledge of the Bible is necessary, our personal, loving involvement with other people is just as necessary to keep us on the right track. It's one thing to know right from wrong; it's quite another to have one or more close friends talk things over with you, encourage you, share your difficult times, and lovingly correct you when they see you continuing in a pattern that is apt to hurt you. For this reason, the Bible places great stress on caring relationships with other Christians. Paul recognized the role that mutual love of Christians for each other played in helping us get rid of our hang-ups:

"And may the Lord make your love to grow and overflow to each other and to everyone else, just as our love does toward you. This will result in your hearts being made strong, sinless, and holy by God our Father, so that you may stand before him guiltless on that day when our Lord Jesus Christ returns with all those who belong to him" (1 Thessalonians 3:12-13, *TLB*).

Here Paul actually says loving relationships help make us more spiritual. While biblical knowledge is the foundation of the Christian's life, maturity doesn't come without deep personal relations. The Bible makes this clear in many places. Although it contains many guides for positive living, we can briefly discuss five specific ways we are instructed to help each other.

### Setting the Broken Bone

In Galatians 6:1 Paul wrote, "Brethren, even if a man is caught in any trespass, you who are spiritual restore such a one in a spirit of gentleness; looking to yourself, lest you too be tempted." Paul tells us here that we have a responsibility to "restore" a Christian friend who has fallen into wrongdoing. The word restore is the Greek word *katartizo*. It was used of a doctor setting a broken bone, and the verb tense implies a restoration process that takes time. The picture here is one Christian assisting a sinning brother· to overcome his sin. In doing this we are to remember that we, too, have faults and can just as easily fail. This attitude, of course, is vital. If we try to correct others with an arrogant sense of superiority, we will only arouse their resentments and make the problem worse.

### Bearing the Burden

Paul then goes on to say, "Bear one another's burdens, and thus fulfill the law of Christ" (Galatians 6:2, *NASB*). The word "burden" is the Greek word *baros.* It is used to describe an object that is heavy and oppressive. When we face a burdensome problem such as a death in the family, a devastating financial reversal, a teenage runaway, or a divorce, we must not be too proud to allow others to help us carry the burden. We must also be sensitive to others' needs and be there to help when they have a burden. The way life usually goes, each of us will hit a few times when others must help us with the load. At other times we will be free enough from our own burdens to be able to help those who are now under heavy pressure.

A few verses later Paul makes an apparently contradictory statement: "For each one shall bear his own load" (6:5, *NASB*). Here the word "load" (wrongly translated "burden" in the King James Version) is the Greek word *phortion.* It simply means an object (not necessarily burdensome) that is to be carried. We all have responsibilities that we are to carry by ourselves. Earning a living and supporting a family aren't regarded as "burdens" in the Bible. For a mother to devote herself to her children and keep house or for a student to do his homework—are not considered burdens. We are sufficiently capable and expected to do them for ourselves.

### Confronting the Unruly

In another helpful statement Paul says, "And we urge you, brethren, admonish the unruly, encourage the fainthearted, help the weak, be patient with all men" (1 Thessalonians 5:14, *NASB*). Here Paul spells out more clearly how we are to help each other.

Paul begins by telling us to *admonish* the unruly. The Greek word *noutheteo* is a Greek present tense that means this process must be repeated often. It literally means to "put in mind," and usually implies a reprimand or a rebuke—at least a mild confrontation. In First Corinthians

4:14 Paul says to the Corinthians: "I do not write these things to shame you, but to admonish you as my beloved children" (*NASB*). He shows here how we are to confront and rebuke each other—in real love.

Paul makes clear, however, that "admonishing" is not "shaming." "Shaming," in the Greek, meant to "hang the head." It implied humiliation. When people are being selfish, unthoughtful, irresponsible, or are guilty of other sins, they are not to be humiliated, as the Pharisees tried to do to the adulterous woman when they brought her before Jesus (John 8). They are to be *admonished* with love.

We should also notice whom Paul says we are to admonish: they are "the unruly." This is a Greek word that meant to be "out of step" and was applied to soldiers. More specifically, it came to be applied to those who refused to work—some have suggested the word "loafer" as a better translation. Certain Thessalonian Christians were "freeloading" and Paul says they should be admonished to get in step.

We must be careful about whom we are admonishing. Some people are aggressively rebellious and need a strong confrontation. Without a clear-cut admonishing they won't listen. Other people are very different; they are sensitive and easily hurt. If we rebuke them strongly we may push them deeper into depression. To these people Paul gives us a different instruction.

### Encouraging the Fainthearted

Paul says we should "*encourage* the fainthearted." The word "encourage" is the Greek word *paramutheo*. It was an emotional type of word used for comforting the bereaved. The Thessalonian church was undergoing persecution, and some were less courageous than others. The pressures of life were starting to overwhelm them. Paul says to comfort and encourage them—show them plenty of support and love as they need it. Note that Paul does *not* say "encourage the unruly" or "admonish the fainthearted." The unruly are the ones that need admonishing. The fainthearted need encouragement.

We cannot stress enough the importance of having the right medicine for the right illness. Not everyone with a problem needs confrontation, and not everyone in trouble needs encouragement. We must be sensitive to the needs of others and give the right aid to the right patient.

### Holding on to the Weak

Next Paul says, "Hold on to the weak." The word "hold on" is the Greek word *antexō*, "to hold fast." Jesus used this word in Luke 16:13 when he said, "No servant can serve two masters; for either he will hate the one and love the other, or else he will *hold to* one and despise the other" (*NASB*). Who were the weak? Probably the spiritually weaker, less mature people who could easily be driven away from the fellowship of Christians by persecution or else fall back into previous sins. Instead of despising them and considering them weaklings, we are to stick with them through thick and thin, and eventually bring them to maturity.

## What Makes Grace Work

The few verses we have just looked at in detail could be multiplied over and over from the teachings of the New Testament. Christians are commanded to "exhort" one another (Hebrews 3:13), "comfort" one another (1 Thessalonians 4:18—same Greek word as "exhort" but used differently here), "pray for" one another (James 5:16), confess our sins to one another (James 5:16), love one another (John 13:34) and serve one another (Galatians 5:13). Churches were also to remove immoral members and forbid them from coming, and Christians were to refuse even to associate with other Christians who continued in serious sin after much exhortation (1 Thessalonians 5:14, 15). One could hardly imagine a more intensely personal community than this! The close personal relationships, the mutual burden bearing, admonishing, and comforting were the machinery that made grace work.

### Personal Concern Versus Impersonal Codes

This is the alternative to legalism. If we teach freedom without this personal corrective force, we will have license. And if we set up a system of external controls instead of a caring involvement with one another we're back under law.

Some regulations are necessary for any church or organization, but they should be kept to a minimum. The biblical pattern for correcting Christians isn't to establish more regulations; it's to lovingly and honestly confront the sinning brother. When Paul discovered the Corinthians were living licentiously, he rebuked them for their bad attitudes and exhorted them to love and holiness. He told them to get back to biblical standards, but he didn't add new ideas of his own. When we are on the receiving end of mature instruction and correction, we begin to experience the love and concern of others for us. This is a much greater stimulus to change than an impersonal set of regulations.

The twentieth century world is lonely, impersonal, indifferent, and afraid. A truly Christian island of personal concern in this great impersonal sea would be so attractive that many non-Christians could not resist it. And it would certainly be a great, life-changing force in the experience of many. Twentieth-century Christianity needs a good dose of this first-century heritage!

## 15

# "But That's Not Where My Head Is!"

For some months I had counseled a young businessman. During one session he said he knew all about God's love and grace and had heard about it for years. But although he knew these teachings, he still had trouble feeling God accepted him. At one point he said, "Man, I know all that jazz about God's love and grace, but I can't feel it. That's not where my head is at!" To be more accurate, we might rephrase his words: "Man, I know all that jazz about God's love and grace, but that's not where my *heart* is at!" It's one thing to *know* about God's love and grace, it's quite another to *feel* them. At one time or another most of us feel God is distant from us and does not accept us. In fact, most of us go through predictable cycles of feelings in the Christian life.

### What's Your Route?

When we first come to Christ, most of us are genuinely excited. We feel clean, forgiven, loved, and reconciled. A spontaneous Christian life seems to well up from within. We want to read our Bibles, attend church, and share with other Christians.

150

### The Mountain-Valley Routine

But slowly the enthusiasm begins to wear off. Perhaps we have taken on a steady diet of responsibilities in the church. What was fun at first now seems like a duty. Bible reading becomes dull and prayer turns into ritual. Besides this, we have committed a number of sins since we became Christians and we start forgetting God has already paid the price. Gradually guilt begins to grow. We know we should be excited, but we aren't.

About this time we go to a religious retreat and get some new insight into the Christian life. We either come to a deeper understanding of our forgiveness or make a new commitment to the Lord. We think, "This is it" and we charge "down the mountain" with a sense of vitality and vigor. The joy we had when we first became Christians has returned and now we're back on the right track. We have gotten rid of our guilt emotions and are feeling fine.

For a time everything goes well, but after a while we notice we've slipped back into the old patterns. We start feeling we aren't quite as good a Christian as we ought to be and our guilt begins to grow again. After a time we might attend another retreat and get fired up again. But soon the pattern is repeated. It seems like we're on a "spiritual roller coaster."

### Safe In the Religious Rut

After a few experiences like this, many of us become disillusioned. We're not sure whether the problem is ours or God's, but we're tired of this up and down approach. Knowing that the Christian life is important, we don't want to throw it off entirely. But neither do we want to keep getting our hopes up only to be let down again. After a few months or years of this we are firmly planted in a religious rut. We may go to church. We may read our Bibles. And we look like "fine Christians" to other people. But somehow our vital Christian experience is only a memory of the past.

When we hear a message on God's grace and freedom, we start to get up our hopes. But suddenly we remember what has happened in the past. The thought comes, "Suppose it doesn't work? I'll just be disillusioned again." Not wanting a mountain-valley experience, we choose the safe thing. We just stay like we are. We reason, "I know some people talk about a thrilling Christian life and I wish I had it, but it doesn't work for me. Besides that, at least I'm not at the other end. I am a Christian and things are going pretty good. I guess I'll settle to be average."

This is where multitudes of long-time church members and their children are. The children may have grown up in Christian homes and gone to Christian schools, but it's all become a routine cultural experience. They are safe but dead. Someone has said they are the "frozen chosen." They are really *afraid* to change.

### "Whee, I'm Free!"

Some people have a different reaction. After struggling with the Christian life awhile they come across some teachings on God's grace. Immediately they start to loosen up. Where they may have been regular church attenders, they now start catching up on their sleep Sunday mornings. Whereas they used to study the Bible almost daily, they now go for long periods without looking at it. And where their external conduct has been above reproach, they now start dabbling in some overt sins.

This poses a very complex problem. Bible reading, prayer, and joining other Christians in worship and right living are important. Yet upon beginning to understand the wideness of God's grace, some people stop some of their good habits and give the impression that God's grace leads to ir-responsible living.

### We Look on the Outside

Actually, this person's rebellious feelings and attitudes were always there—they were just covered over with a coating of Christian conformity. Although he may have profitted some from his Christian activities, he didn't really enjoy reading his Bible, praying, or attending church. If he had, he would have continued with them after he saw his freedom. His Christian life was mainly duty. When the duty motive was removed and fear expelled, he had nothing left to motivate him. His true self started to come out.

This bothers us at first because, quite frankly, we usually prefer compliant, quiet, non-troublesome church members. Even when rebellion, pride, depression, lust, and a host of wrong motivations lie just beneath the surface, we feel better with outwardly conforming people.

Imagine you were a minister. Would you rather have members of your congregation who occasionally showed their intemperance by getting drunk or have the same number of people who are overweight? Would you rather have a rebellious adolescent who takes his anger out on God or a faithful one who keeps her feelings in and suffers from depression? Would you rather have an elder guilty of extra-marital affair or have the same man hide his feelings of lust and sing in the choir on Sunday mornings? Obviously, most of us would much prefer the more acceptable behavior.

Fortunately, God isn't content with this superficial type of Christian conformity. He wants to root out the inner thoughts that lie behind the overt acts. In fact, he will sometimes put us in situations where the rebellion comes out and shakes us, just to move us off dead center.

Since we have acted out of fear motives for so long, we sometimes find it difficult to believe God doesn't really motivate by threats or fear. It's much like a child whose parent says, "I'll love you no matter what you do!" Sometimes the child wants to find out if the parent really means it, so he does something really bad to test the parent. We can try the same with God. When we hear he accepts us completely as we are and will never get angry or punish us, we can't quite believe it. We act out a few sins just to see if it's really true. It takes time to understand that God really does forgive us and that he really intends for us to be free. Then we can move into meaningful routines of Christian life. What used to be "ruts of routine" have turned to "grooves of grace!"

## Toward Freedom and Stability

The Bible has answers to all these frustrating experiences in the Christian life. It speaks to those who go from mountain peak to the valley, it speaks to those who are stuck in a religious rut, and it counsels those who say, "Whee! I'm free!" It seeks to move us beyond these immature experiences down the road toward lasting, stable freedom. Much of this growth involves reeducating our conscience and overcoming guilt.

### *Reeducating Your Conscience*

The long course of childhood leaves deep imprints on us all. Our self-concepts, our ideal-selves, and our corrective-selves are so ingrained that a brief encounter with the thought that we are to like ourselves and be free of guilt doesn't suddenly overcome years of feeling otherwise.

Although a fresh understanding of God's grace may bring a great new sense of spontaneity and freedom—a mountaintop experience—it takes much more to keep our newfound freedom growing. We need to see lasting changes in both our ideals and our ways of motivating ourselves to grow.

To begin with, the standards of our ideal-self must be brought in line with the Bible. If our conscience is overeducated and we feel guilty about things the Bible doesn't say are sin, we must learn to reject those extra-biblical standards and focus only on God's expectations for us. If our ideal-self is under-educated and we are used to rationalizing God's standards away, we must educate our ideals upward. We must learn to call a spade a spade. If God calls something sin we shouldn't call it otherwise.

In the same way, our punitive- and corrective-selves must change. We must learn that the guilt motivations of the punitive self never come from God. We must learn to realize these accusations are stimulated by the devil. And we must learn to experience the constructive sorrow that comes from a loving corrective-self. We must stop mentally punishing ourselves and learn to speak to ourselves with respect and love.

But this isn't easy. In fact, this process will take a lifetime. None of us will ever have our ideals identical with God's. None of us will ever be entirely free of guilt. And none of us will ever be totally loving with ourselves and others. Man's fall and our rebellion have left indelible imprints on us. But we can make great strides in overcoming the inhibiting bonds of guilt. To do it, God has given us two types of help.

### *"The Good Book"*

Our first resource for overcoming guilt is the Bible. In it we have all of God's ideals. David wrote:

"Thy word I have treasured in my heart, that I may not sin against thee. I will meditate on thy precepts, and regard thy ways. I shall delight in thy statutes; I shall not forget thy word" (Psalm 119:11, 15, 16, *NASB*).

David says he repeatedly meditates on God's instructions. He hides them in his heart and they become an integral part of his life. To use our modern psychological terminology, we might say that as David studied the Bible, it gradually became a part of his ideal-self. The Bible corrected David's false notions of what was good for him and replaced them with the truths of God's plan for his life. We all need this same correction and it won't come apart from the Bible. Although God uses people to instruct and correct us, the only completely trustworthy source for our ideals is the Bible.

We also have clear teachings on the proper motives for overcoming sin and the resolution of the guilt feelings coming from our punitive corrective-self. Writing to the Christians at Ephesus, Paul said:

"And you were dead in your trespasses and sins. . . . But God, being rich in mercy, because of his great love with which he loved us, even when we were dead in our transgressions, made us alive together with Christ (by grace you have been saved), and raised us up with him, and seated us with him in the heavenly places, in Christ Jesus, in order that in the ages to come he might show the surpassing riches of his grace in kindness toward us in Christ Jesus. . . .

"I, therefore, the prisoner of the Lord, entreat you to walk in a manner worthy of the calling with which you have been called, with all humility and gentleness, with patience, showing forbearance to one another in love, being diligent to preserve the unity of the Spirit in the bond of peace" (Ephesians 2:1, 4-7; 4:1-3, *NASB*).

Here Paul gives us the true motive for self correction and shows how our beliefs should tie to our actions. God has chosen us, rescued us from our sins, and is preparing us for eternity with him. In response to this great love and provision, we should be willing to put off our former rebellious ways of life and humbly develop new patterns of thought and action.

There is no hint here of a hostile, punitive type of guilt motivation. The Bible gives us clear instructions for self correction but it also sets the pattern completely in the context of God's love.

### The Good People

As the creator of our personalities, God made another provision for our growth. It is the relationships we have with other people. God didn't choose to put each of us on a separate island, place a Bible in our hand, and tell us to grow! Instead, he created us as social beings and he planned the family and church structure to meet our needs for emotional support and spiritual growth.

At the very moment of creation, God planned to have people meet each other's needs. He looked at Adam and said, "It is not good for the man to be alone; I will make him a helper suitable for him" (Genesis 2:18, *NASB*). In other places the Bible tells us that husbands are to love their wives, parents are to lovingly correct their children, older women are to instruct the younger, and all Christians are to love each other (Ephesians 5:28; 6:4; Titus 2:4; John 15:12).

Behind these relationships is a dual purpose. God wants us not only to meet each other's needs, but also to offer a picture of God to others. John wrote, "Dear friends, since God loved us as much as that, we surely ought to love each other too. For though we have never yet seen God, when we love each other God lives in us and his love within us grows ever stronger" (1 John 4:11, 12, *TLB*). In the same chapter he wrote, "For the one who does not love his brother whom he has seen, cannot love God whom he has not seen" (4:20b, *NASB*).

Here John makes a vital point—the way we relate to others is a training ground for relating to God. If we are always suspicious of people and can never trust them, we are apt to transfer the same attitude toward God. But if we learn we can trust people, we find it easier to trust God! If our childhood experiences have programmed us to expect rejection, punishment, and criticism, but Christian friends give us love, acceptance, and wise correction, we begin to change our expectations. We can begin to believe that God feels the same way about us. This causes the strength of our punitive-self to wane, and the loving corrective-self to grow strong in its place. We now begin to understand God doesn't make us feel guilty, but motivates us by love.

### The Power of "Honey, I Forgive You"

I had a clear demonstration of this in a group counseling session. After much struggle a woman in her thirties began talking about a sexual sin from her teen-age years. Ever since that time she'd felt guilty and had been unable to accept God's forgiveness. After tearfully recounting the instance she looked fearfully at her husband. He got up from his chair, walked over and put his arms around her and said with much emotion, "Honey, I forgive you." From that moment on she was able to feel God's forgiveness. Although she still had to occasionally battle with her punitive-self attitudes, her husband's forgiveness had accomplished what years of prayer and confession had failed to do.

In like ways, each of us represents God to one another.

This is one reason the Bible stresses the importance of close relationships with other Christians. We are to become a source of each other's new ideals. And as we are lovingly forgiven and corrected we begin to see how God might do the same. When we "confess our faults to each other and pray for each other" we gain a deeper sense of the reality of God's love and forgiveness.

### We Can Change!

Even though we have long years of bad emotional habits, they can be changed. As we cement the truths of God's forgiveness in our minds and as we experience the daily acceptance of our friends, we gradually begin to change. This is one of the most important aspects of professional counseling. When people have problems they can't seem to get a handle on, it is good for them to have another help them with it. A qualified professional counselor is skilled in helping people understand the causes of their poor self-concepts and guilt emotions and learn to overcome these negative emotions. People who can't seem to get free of these inhibiting feelings should feel free to turn to a professionally trained person to help them overcome their guilt.

At this point some people say, "But that doesn't sound right. If I'm a Christian, why can't I just pray about it and let God solve my problem?" Though this is a common feeling, it is completely false. The Bible doesn't say we are to "tell it to Jesus alone." To refuse to seek another's help when God has appointed such a way is false pride. The Bible says, "Therefore, confess your sins *to one another,* and pray for one another, so that you may be healed" (James 5:16, *NASB*).

Paul repeatedly says that deep relationships with other people are actually one of God's ways of making us strong and whole. He writes, "The more you go on this way [loving others deeply] the more you will grow strong spiritually and become fruitful and useful to our Lord Jesus Christ" (2 Peter 1:8, *TLB*).

The Bible doesn't say we should run around telling our problems to everyone we meet, but it does say we should "bear each other's burdens," "confess our faults," and "pray for each other." When we fail to do this, it's usually because we are afraid of others knowing our inner feelings. We think they might reject us or lose faith in us. We rationalize our dishonesty by saying, "I want to set a good example," or "They can't really help." But these are just disguises. If we are to follow God's designs, we will move beyond our fears and pride, step down off our pedestals and become real, feeling people. This is exactly what we must do if we are to grow. As we learn we can be ourselves and yet be accepted by our friends, we grasp the depth of God's forgiveness and acceptance.

None of us, of course, will reach perfection in this life. But change and growth are not beyond our grasp. This is what the New Testament is all about. God wants us to know that we *can* let loose of the ravages of guilt. We *can* learn to accept ourselves. We *can* begin to experience meaningful and happy lives. And we *can* taste real freedom here and now. We don't have to wait until we get to heaven.

When Jesus gave his first sermon in his hometown of Nazareth, he quoted Isaiah's prophecy about the Messiah and applied it to himself. He said, "He has sent me to proclaim release to the captives . . . to set free those who are downtrodden" (Luke 4:18, *NASB*). In another sermon he said, "And ye shall know the truth, and the truth shall make you free" (John 8:32). That is the message of this book. Jesus Christ lived and died to release us from captivity to our hangups and our sins. As we apply his truth we can be free!